Framework
FOCUS

D0189352

Drama

Matthew O'Neill
Jo O'Neill

Published by Letts Educational
The Chiswick Centre
414 Chiswick High Road
London W4 5TF

(t) 020 89963333
(f) 020 87428390
(e) mail@lettsed.co.uk
(w) www.letts-education.com

Letts Educational Limited is a division of Granada Learning Limited, part of Granada plc.

First published 2003

ISBN 1 84085 8761

British Library Cataloguing in Publication Data
A catalogue record for this book is available from the British Library.

Developed and packaged by McLean Press Ltd

Commissioned by Helen Clark

Project management by Vicky Butt and Julia Swales

Edited by Jo Kemp

Cover design by bigtop, Bicester, UK

Internal design by bigtop, Bicester, UK

Illustrations by James Arnold, Linda Combi, Serena Curmi, Nick Duffy, Rosalind Hudson, Paul McCaffrey and Andrew Quelch

Production by PDQ

Printed and bound in Italy by G. Canale & C., Turin

Acknowledgements
The authors and publishers wish to thank the following for permission to use copyright material:
Alan Brodie Representation Ltd on behalf of the author for an extract from John Godber, *Teechers*, p. 3. Copyright © 1987 John Godber; David Calcutt for an extract from *The Terrible Fate of Humpty Dumpty* by David Calcutt, Nelson (1986) p. 17; Curtis Brown Ltd, London, on behalf of the author's Estate for an extract from John Steinbeck, *The Grapes of Wrath* (1975); HarperCollins Publishers for extracts from Kelvin Reynolds and Adrian Lockwood, *You Made Me*, Plays Plus Series, Collins Educational (2000) pp. 45, 46; and Nigel Gray, *Black Harvest*, Plays Plus Series, Collins Educationl (1986); David Higham Associates on behalf of the author for extracts from Anne Fine, *The Granny Project*, Plays Plus Series, Collins Educational; Hodder & Stoughton Publishers for Andrew and Polly Fusek Peters, 'Slugs and Snails and Puppy Dog Tails' and 'Sugar and Spice and All Things Nice' from *Poems With Attitude* by Andrew and Polly Fusek Peters, Hodder Wayland (2000); Methuen Publishing Ltd for an extract from Willy Russell, *Blood Brothers*, pp. 22–3; Oxford University Press for an extract from Gillian Cross, *The Demon Headmaster*, adapted by Adrian Flynn, pp. 16–18; Penguin Books Ltd for extracts from Zlata Filipovic, *Zlata's Diary: A Child's Life in Sarajevo*, trans. Christina Pribichevich-Zoric, Viking (1994) (first published in France as Le Journal de Zlata , Fixot et editions Robert Laffont, 1993). Copyright © Zlata Filipovic, 1993, 1994; Michelle Magorian, *Goodnight Mister Tom*, Kestrel (1981). Copyright © Michelle Magorian, 1981; Anton Chekhov, 'The Proposal' from *Plays* by Anton Checkhov, trans. Elisaveta Fen, Penguin (1951). Translation Copyright © Eilisaveta Fen, 1951, 1954; and Sophocles, 'Antigone' from *The Theban Plays* by Sophocles, trans. E F Watling, Penguin Classics (1947). Copyright © E F Watling, 1947; PFD on behalf of the authors for Wendy Cope, 'Tich Miller' from *Making Cocoa for Kingsley Amis* by Wendy Cope, Faber and Faber; and Roger McGough, 'Nooligan' from *You at the Back: Selected Poems 1967–1987* by Roger McGough, Jonathan Cape (1991); The Random House Group Ltd for extracts from Robert Swindells, *Room 13*, Corgi Yearling (1989); and Ian McEwan, *The Daydreamer*, Jonathan Cape (1994) pp. 1–2, 54–5; Philip Ridley for 'The Prince and the Snail'; Vernon Scannell for 'A Case of Murder'; Caroline Sheldon Literary Agency on behalf of the author for John Agard, 'Way Out Mum, Way Way Out Dad'; Time Warner Books UK for Maya Angelou, 'Life Doesn't Frighten Me' from *And Still I Rise* by Maya Angelou, Virago (1978). Copyright © 1978 by Maya Angelou.

Every effort has been made to trace the copyright holders but if any have been inadvertently overlooked the publishers will be pleased to make the necessary arrangement at the first opportunity.

Contents

KEY TO ENGLISH FRAMEWORK TEACHING OBJECTIVES
SL = Speaking and Listening   R = Reading

Introduction

Framework Focus Drama is a collection of lessons that cover the specific Drama learning objectives of the National Literacy strategy for English in KS3.

The lessons provide opportunities for students to **respond** to texts, to **develop** drama work based on these responses, **present** drama work and **evaluate** their own work and the work of others.

The lessons have clear aims that relate closely to the drama objectives. They begin with a starter activity that aims to begin the lesson quickly and with pace. The starter activity will lead into or relate to the main learning activity. Each lesson is based around a text that has a strong sense of character or clear narrative. The learning objectives are covered through a series of practical tasks and are reflected on in a review or plenary activity. Students are asked to assess their own learning and the reviews provide assessment opportunities for teachers. Homework tasks that extend or reinforce learning are built in to lessons where appropriate.

Students are regularly asked to assess their understanding or effective demonstration of skills through a number system 1–5.

1 indicates beginning to understand

2 indicates some understanding

3 indicates good understanding

4 indicates very good understanding

5 indicates complete confidence with the concept.

The same number system can be applied when students are assessing the effectiveness of others' drama work.

The lessons are written to communicate directly with the student. Teachers can use this in a variety of ways; allowing students to manage their own learning through the lesson or by applying their own voice to the lesson and managing learning more directly.

The lessons can be worked through sequentially as a drama scheme of work, or they can be used selectively as part of an English programme of study. The lessons work as well in the English classroom as they do in the Drama studio.

The glossary provides a range of specialist drama terms, which will allow students to begin talking about their drama work in an articulate and meaningful way. Using specialist drama terminology will prepare students for the demands of KS3 Standard Assessment Task in English and will be a good foundation for study of Drama at GCSE level.

These lessons have been tried and tested in a variety of schools by experienced English and Drama teachers, Newly Qualified Teachers and student teachers on teaching practice. They provide lessons with pace, interest and clear learning objectives – and students enjoy them.

Matthew O'Neill & Jo O'Neill

Review of KS2 Drama (1)

Aims

- To review what you learnt in drama in Years 5 and 6.
- To get to know some of your new class mates and to develop your group work skills in this new class.

Starter session

- As a whole class, stand in a circle. Take it in turns to say your name loud and clear to the class. Then tell the class something you like doing. Now do an action that shows you doing the thing you enjoy.
- Once you have said your name and done the action, the class repeats it all together.
  e.g. 'My name is Spike and I like riding my bike.'
  All: 'His name is Spike and he likes riding his bike.'
  Now it is the next person's turn.
- Go all the way round the circle. By the time you get to the end you should know quite a few names.

Introduction

You may have had a special drama lesson in your primary school or you may have done drama in English or Literacy Hour. Either way, you will have taken part in a wide variety of drama activities and you will have been asked to evaluate your own and others' contributions. In the first two lessons in this book you will be reviewing your learning experiences in drama. In KS3 you will be building on what you have already learnt in KS2.

KEY WORDS

Role-play is when you take on the part of someone else. You aim to see situations as they would and respond as they would.

Development

Complete activities A and B.

 ACTIVITY A

1 In pairs, recollect an amusing story from your primary school.

2 Use this story as a basis for creating a **role-play**.

3 Now act out the role-play for another pair.

4 In fours, evaluate how successful you have been in creating roles, sustaining roles, conveying the action and story of the incident to your audience.

5 Feed back your findings to the class. What did you do well and what would you want to improve?

ACTIVITY B

1 Think about your first few days of secondary school. What are the things that have most and least impressed you? Discuss in groups of four.

2 Imagine you have been commissioned to create a play for Year 6 students at your previous school. The play must convey your first impressions of secondary school.

3 Decide on the characters that will be in the play. What are your dramatic intentions? Rehearse the play, limiting your performance to one minute.

4 Perform your play for the class.

Review

As you watch other people's work, consider the impact the piece would have on a Year 6 audience. What would they feel about coming to secondary school after seeing the play? Feed back your thoughts to the class.

Review of KS2 Drama (2)

Aims

- In this lesson you will be using your knowledge of drama and drama skills to respond to a poem and develop your work into a performance.
- You will be using and identifying drama skills you have developed in Years 5 and 6.

Starter session

- Stand in a circle and take it in turns to say 'hello' around the circle.
- Now say hello around the circle again, but this time say it as if you were:

  1 a lion **2** a mouse **3** a whale **4** a snail **5** an elephant
  6 an ant **7** a tortoise **8** a hare.

- In pairs, consider what you did with your voices to create the animal characteristics.
- Feed back your findings to the group.

ACTIVITY **A**

1 Read the poem silently to yourself.

2 In pairs, take it in turns reading the poem aloud to each other.

3 Now read the poem as a whole class. Taking it in turns to read a single line from the poem, read around the circle until the end.

THE PRINCE AND THE SNAIL

Once, in a castle
a Prince loved a snail.
He painted the shell gold
and kept the snail in his pocket.

The King and the Queen
thought the Prince mad.
'It must be a difficult relationship,'
said the King.
'Why?' asked the Prince.
(Love makes you that way.)

The Queen said,
'Son, let's talk.
You see, there're certain things
you can do
and certain things
you cannot do
and, I'm afraid,
kissing a snail in public
is most definitely out.'

The Prince said to the snail,
'This is hopeless.
We'll have to run away.'
'Mmmm,' said the snail.
(Again, love makes you that way.)

So the Prince ran away
with the golden snail.
They ran to the edge
of the land
and sat on the beach.

'Phew,' said the Prince,
'I'm out of breath.'

'Take me out of you pocket!'
gasped the snail.
'I'm suffocating!'

Then, in the sea,
a huge black monster appeared.
It looked at the Prince
and winked.
'A whale!' said the snail.
'What a flirt!' said the Prince.

That night the Prince
swam out to the whale.
The whale was as big as a castle.
'I love you!' said the Prince.
'Glug, glug!' said the snail.

'Why not live in my belly?'
gurgled the whale.
(You know how whales are.)

So the Prince crawled inside.
'It's dark,' said the Prince.
'I love you,' said the whale.

Once, in a belly,
a Prince loved a whale.
As if the belly were a pocket
and the Prince a golden snail.

By Philip Ridley

ACTIVITY **B**

1 In groups of five, make a small circle. Put your books aside and retell the story from memory around the circle.

2 As a group, decide what the poem is about.

3 Now create a dramatic version of the story from the poem.

4 Cast your play from the group.

5 Use your voice ideas from the starter activity to help you.

6 Rehearse your play in preparation for a performance. As you work, aim to demonstrate your drama knowledge and skills from your work in Years 5 and 6.

Review

Perform your play of 'The Prince and the Snail'. Watch a performance carefully and take note of anything the actors do that helps convey character or **plot**. Feed back your thoughts to the group.

The Daydreamer

Aims

- To develop the drama techniques of **still image** and **thought tracking** to explore, in role, two characters from stories by novelist Ian McEwan.
- To reflect on your own work and the drama work of others.

Starter session

In pairs, spend a minute each recalling a time when you have been day dreaming. Tell your partner about the place where you were, whether anyone else was nearby while you were dreaming, what you should have been doing and what you were dreaming about.

Introduction

Ian McEwan is a well-respected writer of adult fiction; *The Daydreamer* is his first work for young people. You will be using two of his characters, Peter and Barry, as a starting point for your own creative work. You will begin by using still image and will develop your pieces using other drama techniques.

KEY WORDS

Still image is when you create a frozen moment in a scene using your own bodies. You remain completely still as if you have pressed the pause button while watching a video – it is that captured moment. Still image can also be like a statue, created by you or your group to convey an idea or symbolic meaning.

Thought tracking is when you speak a character's thoughts. It is used to reveal the private thoughts that go unspoken. Thought tracking can help you reflect on a moment of action and develop a deeper understanding of character.

Development

Read these two extracts from stories in *The Daydreamer* in which Ian McEwan describes Peter and Barry.

Peter

When Peter Fortune was ten years old grown-up people used to tell him he was a 'difficult' child. He never understood what they meant. He didn't feel difficult at all. He didn't throw milk bottles at the garden wall, or tip tomato ketchup over his head and pretend it was blood, or slash at his granny's ankle with his sword, though he occasionally thought of these things…It was not until he had been a grown-up himself for many years that Peter finally understood. They thought he was difficult because he was so silent. That seemed to bother people.

Barry

What made Barry Tamerlane a successful bully? Peter had given this question a great deal of dreamy thought. His conclusion was there were two reasons for Barry's success. The first was that he seemed able to move in the quickest way between wanting something and having it…The second reason for Tamerlane's success was that everyone was afraid of him.

ACTIVITY A

1 On your own, think of a single word that sums up Peter. Feed your words back to the class. Now do the same thing for Barry.

2 In pairs (one playing Peter, one being Barry), use your bodies to create a still image that could be used to illustrate McEwan's characters.

3 You are now going to create your own characters based on Peter and Barry. Still working in pairs, create three still images that show your characters together (a) at school, (b) on the football field, (c) at a birthday party.

4 Now add a single line of thought tracking for each character to each picture. When thought tracking, speak the thought of the character, not the spoken words they would use.

5 Choose one of the three still images and develop it, using movement and voice, into a short scene showing how your two characters contrast. Start and end your scene with a still image and include a moment of thought tracking, where your character speaks thoughts directly to the audience.

6 Present your pieces quickly to the rest of the class. As you watch each other's work, consider – as a director – what advice you could offer the actors to enhance the contrast between the characters.

ACTIVITY B

1 Which adult characters would be interesting to introduce to the scene? Brainstorm this question as a class.

2 Working in groups of four this time, introduce two new characters into the scene. They should be adults and should communicate the feelings they have for the two children. Use the drama techniques of still image and thought tracking in your devised work.

Review

- Watch one or two of the groups perform their work. In your own group of four reflect on the work you have seen. Think of three elements that were communicated effectively and three areas for improvement. Feed these points back to the groups you have observed.
- Finally, make a judgement on how well you understand the drama techniques of still image and thought tracking. Mark yourself out of five. (Five is the highest and shows you understand fully.)

Bag lady

Aims

- To work **collaboratively** to **devise** a piece of unscripted drama and maintain the attention of your audience when you present your work.
- To develop your speaking skills by experimenting with language in different roles and contexts.

Starter session

- In this exercise you will be starting to build a character, not by what they say, but by how they walk. Half the class observes as the other half walks. Observers decide what the actors are doing to convey character.
- Actors: start walking as yourselves. Find spaces and occasionally change direction. Change your walk to convey the character of: a police officer, a teacher, a soldier, a clown, a priest, a tramp, a bride, a teenager, a builder, a child.
- Observers: feed back to the rest of the class. Now change over, so that observers become walkers and vice versa.

Introduction

Many theatre companies use a process called devising to create a performance. In this process actors and a director will work together, possibly with a writer, to create a play. You will be working in this way to create a story based on two images. You will be conveying the characters and events of the story to an audience.

KEY WORDS

Devise is when you work together to create a performance without a script. You use your own experience of life and drama texts as a starting point in place of a script.

Collaborative working is when members of a group play equal, though possibly different, roles in making a play.

Development

1 Look at Image A. In pairs, create five lines of dialogue that you think this character might hear during the day. Which characters speak these lines? Now create five responses the character might offer.

2 Now look at Image B. In pairs, create five lines of dialogue that the bride might hear through the day. Now think of five responses.

3 Join pairs to make fours. Look at the two pictures. They are very different. Imagine that the bride and the bag lady are the same person at two different moments in her life.

4 Create her story. What has happened in her life to change her circumstances so dramatically?

5 Create four characters that are important to the story. Think back to the starter activity and decide how these characters walk before you think about how they talk. Give the central character a name. Does the way she walks change as her circumstances change?

6 Devise a scene that tells her story. It should show the reason for the change in her life.

7 Run through your scene in a rehearsal and time it. Now select the most important moments in the piece, limiting your performance to one minute.

8 Perform your work to the class. Remember that you are aiming to maintain the attention of the audience.

Review

- In your performance groups, evaluate how well you managed to maintain the attention of your audience. List three things you did that helped you maintain their attention.
- Give yourselves a mark out of five, with five meaning you had their total attention.

Homework

- Look at how a play script is laid out. Try the library.
- Use your devised piece as the basis of your own script writing. Write a script of the most important moment in the scene. Limit your writing to ten lines of dialogue.

A Case of Murder

Aims

- To experiment with the rhythm of language.
- To develop drama techniques to help you anticipate and visualise in your drama work.

Starter session

- Sit or stand in a circle and pass a clap around from one person to the next. You clap when you receive the clap and when you pass it on. Once you are passing the clap rhythmically try changing direction.
- How well did you do in the exercise? What skills do you need to be good at this? How could you get better?

Introduction

Vernon Scannell, poet and one-time boxer, was born in Lincolnshire in 1922. His poem 'A Case of Murder' takes place in a family home. Throughout the poem there is an underlying threat of violence. As you read the poem, enjoy the rhythm and ask yourself what is wrong here.

KEY WORDS

Narrative is the story or plot; the main events, incidents and encounters.

Rehearse (verb) or **rehearsal** (noun) is when you practise a play in preparation for presentation.

Development

1 Complete activities A and B.

1 Read the poem in groups of four. Take it in turns to read it aloud. Read four lines at a time and then swap reader.

A CASE OF MURDER

They should not have left him there alone,
Alone that is except for the cat.
He was only nine, not old enough
To be left alone in a basement flat,
Alone, that is, except for the cat.
A dog would have been a different thing,
A big gruff dog with slashing jaws,
But a cat with round eyes mad as gold,
Plump as a cushion with tucked-in paws —
Better have left him with a fair sized rat!
But what they did was leave him with a cat.
He hated that cat; he watched it sit,
A buzzing machine of soft black stuff,
He sat and watched and he hated it,
Snug in its fur, hot blood in a muff,
And its mad gold star and the way it sat
Crooning dark warmth: he loathed all that.
So he took Daddy's stick and he hit the cat.
Then quick as a sudden crack in glass
It hissed, black flash, to a hiding place
In the dust and dark beneath the coach,
And he followed the grin on his new-made face,
A wide-eyed, frightened snarl of a grin,
And he took the stick and he thrust it in,
Hard and quick in the furry dark.
The black fur squealed and he felt his skin
Prickle with sparks of dry delight.
Then the cat again came into sight,
Shot for the door that wasn't quite shut,
But the boy, quick too, slammed fast the door:
The cat, half-through, was cracked like a nut
And the soft black thud was dumped on the floor.
Then the boy was suddenly terrified
And he bit his knuckles and cried and cried;
But he had to do something with the dead thing there.
His eyes squeezed beads of salty prayer
But the wound of fear gaped wide and raw;
He dared not touch the thing with his hands
So he fetched a spade and shovelled it
And dumped the load of heavy fur
In the spidery cupboard under the stair
Where it's been for years, and though it died
It's grown in that cupboard and its hot low purr
Grows slowly louder year by year:
There'll not be a corner for the boy to hide
When the cupboard swells and all sides split
And the huge black cat pads out of it.

by Vernon Scannell

2 Retell the **narrative** (story) of the poem in your group. From memory, take it in turns to tell a short piece of the narrative. Say no more than ten words, then the next group member carries on.

3 Look at the poem again. Look for clues in the text that might explain the boy's actions.

4 Feed back your findings to the class.

5 What effect does the rhythm of the poem have on the listener?

ACTIVITY **B**

1 In your groups of four, create 'A Day in the Life' of the boy in the poem. The day you create should be the day before he killed the cat. Create a sequence of short scenes in which we see him:
- at home with a parent
- at school with friends
- at school with teachers.

2 As you **rehearse** your work, try to maintain the sense of rhythm that you felt in the starter exercise and heard in the poem. Use it to create a sense of urgency.

3 Present your work to the class.

Review

- What makes people behave violently? Think about the boy in the poem and your own experience. In your group, list five causes of violent behaviour and five ways of avoiding violence.
- Feed back your thoughts to the class.

The Granny Project

Aims

- To respond to the characters, action and events from a scene from Anne Fine's play *The Granny Project*.
- To use drama strategies to anticipate action and resolve problems in **role**.
- To reflect on the impact of your presentations.

Starter session

- In pairs, think about the oldest people you know. Discuss how they live. Think of five words that most accurately reflect their quality of life. Now feed your words back to the class.

Introduction

Anne Fine is a popular novelist. She has adapted many of her novels for the stage. In *The Granny Project* she explores the vexing issue of who should care for the old in a modern family where everyone has busy lives of their own. Ivan is horrified when he finds out that his parents are considering putting Granny in a home.

KEY WORDS

A **role** is a part or character played by an actor.

A **monologue** is where one character speaks directly to the audience.

Development

1 Complete activities A and B.

1 Read the following extract aloud in groups of three.

IVAN   Listen, Nicholas. Do you want to see Granny parcelled off to some Old People's Home, or don't you? You can't have it both ways. You can't make omelettes without breaking eggs. Those two out there mean business. They've had enough. Nine years she's been here, getting steadily worse. They want her out before they're too old to enjoy themselves. But we think she should stay. She's old and feeble and confused. She shouldn't be with strangers. This is her home.

SOPHIE   It's true, Nicholas. They'll send her off to some big strange house that smells of disinfectant all over, and she'll be shoved in a room with three other ancient biddies she's never been introduced to.

IVAN   And if she wanders about getting in everyone's way, like she does here, they'll give her pills to make her so woozy she'll stay in bed.

TANYA   And no one will have time to stop and talk to her, like Mum and Dad do whenever they can stand it.

SOPHIE   We'll be too busy to visit, except at weekends.

TANYA   And in the end, she'll just give up and **die**.

IVAN   And it will be our fault, because we didn't act on our principles and make a stand at the beginning.

2 Is Ivan right? What do you think the characters should do next? Discuss in role what the characters should do next. Continue the scene and develop a plan to save Granny.

3 Create a one-minute scene in which Ivan talks to his mum (Natasha) and dad (Henry) about the problem. Work in threes. What do you think their response to his ideas will be?

1 Now read the next extract in which Natasha responds to Ivan's ideas.

IVAN What do you mean, exactly – do all the caring?
NATASHA *(airily)* Oh, you know. You've seen your father and me do it for nine years. Taking trays in and out ten times a day. Fetching and carrying. Bed changing. Laundering. Medicine giving. Sewing on buttons. Fetching her pension. Buying her peppermints. Changing her television channel. Filling her hot water bottles. Sitting with her for hours. Keeping her room warm. Switching on her lamps when it gets dark and switching them off again when she falls asleep. Tuning her radio. Finding her spectacles. Picking up her book. Closing her window. Opening her window. Drawing her curtains. Writing her few remaining Christmas cards. Consoling her when her friends die. Reminding her to eat…Why are you staring at me? Have I **missed** something?

2 In the play *The Granny Project*, we never see Granny on stage. Working on your own, create a **monologue** in which the character Granny speaks her thoughts and views about how she would like to be cared for in the last years of life. Think about how you would like to be treated.

3 In pairs, take it in turns to perform your monologues to each other.

Review

Were there any moving or interesting moments in the monologues? Report back on any work you have seen that impressed you.

Homework

Research your own family on this issue. Find out how your own parents would like to be looked after when they are old and unable to look after themselves. Be prepared to feed back your findings to the class next lesson.

Room 13

Aims

- To devise and present a scripted piece of drama using the story *Room 13*.
- To develop your work in role to explore the situation and characters of the story.

Starter session

- Working in pairs, describe or remind each other of any school trips you have been on. Can you think of anything that was not meant to happen, or anything unusual?
- Report back some of these stories to the rest of the class.

Introduction

Robert Swindells' spooky story is about a group of children going on a school visit to Whitby in North Yorkshire. Whitby is a real seaside town, famous for its appearance in Bram Stoker's novel, *Dracula*.

In the extract you are about to read, four of the characters, Fliss, Lisa, Gary and Trot are squeezed into the hotel bathroom at midnight. They are keeping watch over the cupboard door next to room 12, because some peculiar things are happening to one of their friends and they believe the answer lies in the cupboard.

KEY WORDS

Dialogue is where two or more characters are speaking in a scene.

Development

1 Read the passage carefully on your own.

Presently they heard the distant chimes again. Midnight. They looked at one another and drifted towards the door. As they did so, Lisa let out a stifled cry and pointed. 'Look.' They looked. The cupboard was room thirteen.

'Oh, wow,' moaned Gary. 'It's real. I thought it was a dream, but it's real.'

'You scared then?' Trot's words carried a challenge, but his voice came out a croak.

'I told you, didn't I?' breathed Fliss. 'I told you it wasn't a dream.'

'Oh, Fliss,' whimpered Lisa. 'Oh, my God, what am I doing here?' Fliss put an arm round her friend and squeezed. 'It's OK, Lisa. Take it easy. It's just a door with a number on it, right? We don't have to go in there or anything. We don't even have to go near it, for goodness sake.' She looked at the others. 'What now?'

'Listen!' Trot was watching the stairs. 'I think someone's coming.'

'Oh, no!' Gary crammed all of his fingers in his mouth and stood, gazing at the stair-top and shaking his head.

There came the unmistakable sound of footfalls slowly ascending, and a pale shape came into view.

2 Working in groups of four, discuss the extract. Which adjectives would you use to describe the emotions or reactions of the characters?

3 Now each of you adopt one of the four characters. Read through the extract again, reading aloud your own character's **dialogue**. Try to convey the feelings of the character as the author suggests, e.g. 'moaned Gary', 'whimpered Lisa'.

4 Evaluate one another's work and make helpful suggestions as to how the characters can be more convincingly played.

5 Try the piece again, but this time add the movements and facial expressions of each character. Some of these are suggested by the author. Do not forget that they are huddled together in a small bathroom!

6 Rehearse your piece several times and try to learn the lines and actions. You will find it much easier and more effective if you do not have to look at the text.

Review

- Each group presents their work to the class.
- As an audience, evaluate how effectively each group conveyed the feelings of the characters and the tense situation in which they found themselves.
- Remember that it is important to evaluate your own work too. Give yourself a mark out of five, with five being the highest mark.

No more Humpty Dumpty

Aims

- To explore in role and respond to an extract from the play *The Terrible Fate of Humpty Dumpty*.
- To respond to the play, interpreting the action, characters and events.
- To work with others to devise a piece of drama for an audience.

Starter session

- Imagine for a moment that you are a parent. Thinking in role, what do you worry about as your child leaves you in the morning to go to school?
- Speak out your thoughts, still in role, to the class.
- In groups of four, discuss which worries are likely to happen to children and which are unlikely.
- Feed back your findings to the whole class.

Introduction

The Terrible Fate of Humpty Dumpty was written by playwright David Calcutt. He worked collaboratively with young people, improvising and devising work which was the basis of the characters and events in the play. The play begins with the tragic death of Terry Dumpton and then follows the investigation into his death.

KEY WORDS

Improvisation is when you devise and present a storyline with little preparation.

Flashbacks are scenes that show something that has happened in the past.

Development

1 Read aloud to yourself Mrs Dumpton's monologue; she is addressing the audience directly.

MRS DUMPTON   We couldn't get anything out of him. He'd always been such a happy child. Quiet, but happy. We'd always got on well together as a family. You know, of course, that Mr Dumpton has got a police record. He was inside for a year. It was silly, really. He got mixed up in something. But he'd served his time. That's why we moved to a new area, to try and leave all that behind. Start a new life. Then all this trouble started with Terry. If only he'd have talked to us, told us about what was happening, then this ... this might not have happened. I heard him crying quite a few times as well. In his bedroom at night. But when I went in to see him, he just pretended to be asleep. That's not normal, is it? For a boy of his age to cry in bed at night. And then there was the whole thing about the money. That shocked me more than anything, I can tell you.

2 In pairs, select five words from the extract that convey 'family life' for the Dumptons. Now add five words of your own that describe the atmosphere in the family.

3 Select in your pairs one incident that Mrs. Dumpton describes in her monologue. Think about this incident and decide which roles you will play. Develop this scene through **improvisation** in role.

4 **Flashbacks** are used in the play to build a picture of what happened to Terry Dumpton. Now join your pair with two other pairs to make a group of six. Link the three improvisations together as flashbacks.

5 Present your work to the class.

Review

- Discuss in your groups of six Mrs Dumpton's worries. What are the similarities between these worries and the worries of your own parents?
- Feed back your findings to the class.

Homework

Research in role: You are a parent and you suspect your child is being bullied.

- What advice would you give your child?
- Write five bullet points detailing the advice.
- Ask your parents or carers what advice they would give. Do you agree with their ideas?

Goodnight Mister Tom

Aims

- To learn the techniques of **thought tunnel** and improvisation to explore through role-play the theme of evacuation, using Michelle Magorian's novel *Goodnight Mister Tom*.
- To experiment with the language used by the different characters in the novel.

Starter session

- Brainstorm as a whole class what the word *evacuee* means.
- Consider why children were evacuated during the Second World War.
- On your own, write a short list of the special belongings (other than clothes) that you would pack in your suitcase if you had to be evacuated suddenly from your home. Remember that you have to carry your own case!
- Compare your list with a partner.
- Keep your list for use later.

Introduction

Goodnight Mister Tom is the story of the evacuation of young Willie Beech from London to a small country village in 1939. He is left in the care of Tom Oakley, a man whose wife and child have died some years before, leaving him grumpy, unsociable and reluctant to look after a young boy.

KEY WORDS

Thought tunnel – when a character from the drama walks slowly between two rows of students. You link your hands together in the air to create an arch. As the character passes each student they call out what they think the character is thinking.

Mime – a performance that conveys character and plot using movement and gesture, without the use of words.

Development

1 Complete activities A and B.

1 Read the following extract on your own.

> Tom took a second look at the child. The boy was thin and sickly-looking, pale with limp sandy hair and dull grey eyes.
>
> 'His name's Willie,' said the woman.
>
> Willie, who had been staring at the ground, looked up. Round his neck, hanging from a piece of string, was a cardboard label. It read 'William Beech'.
>
> Tom was well into his sixties, a healthy, robust, stockily-built man with a head of thick white hair. Although he was of average height, in Willie's eyes he was a towering giant with skin like coarse, wrinkled brown paper and a voice like thunder.
>
> He glared at Willie. 'You'd best come in,' he said abruptly.
>
> The woman gave a relieved smile. 'Thank you so much,' she said, and she backed quickly away and hurried down the tiny path towards the other children. Willie watched her go.

2 Decide what Willie is feeling as he stands on Tom's doorstep. What concerns him most about his new life?

3 In pairs, speak your thoughts to your partner.

4 As a whole class, create a thought tunnel for Willie to walk through. To do this, one person takes on the role of Willie, the rest of the class makes two lines and forms a tunnel by linking their hands. Willie then walks slowly through the tunnel imagining he is walking to Mister Tom's door for the first time. As Willie passes you in the tunnel, speak Willie's thoughts.

5 Find a space on your own now. Using the list you made earlier, imagine that you are being evacuated and are packing your case. **Mime** this piece of work.

6 Working with a partner, imagine the two of you are sitting on a train. You have not met before but are both being evacuated to the same village.

7 Improvise three lines of dialogue each. Remember that you will have just said goodbye to loved ones whom you may not see again for quite a while and you have probably never stayed in the country before.

8 Present some of these scenes to the rest of the class.

ACTIVITY **B**

1 In groups of three, recreate and develop the scene in the extract using the characters Willie, Tom and the woman (Billeting Officer). You can use the lines of dialogue given, but you must use improvisation to include the beginning of the scene and what happens when Tom and Willie enter the house together for the first time.

2 Run through the scene again. This time, pay particular attention to the language and tone of voice you use for your character. Remember the following:

● Tom is an abrupt man, over sixty. He has a country dialect.
● Willie is a shy and scared boy.
● The Billeting Officer is 'a harassed middle-aged woman'.

Review

● Present these scenes to the class.
● As an audience, evaluate how well the actors managed to adopt the age and emotions of their character through their voices, language and movements.
● Evaluate your understanding of the thought tunnel technique.
● Give yourself a mark out of five, with five indicating a full understanding of the technique.

Macbeth

Aims

- To experiment with Shakespeare's language in the roles of Macbeth and Lady Macbeth.
- To start to develop drama techniques for problem-solving.

Starter session

- With a partner, describe an occasion when a friend or brother or sister got you into trouble by persuading you to do something that you did not want to do.
- Explain your partner's story to the class. Your partner then describes why they allowed themselves to be persuaded.

Introduction

Macbeth, believed to have been written in 1605, is one of William Shakespeare's best-known tragedies. It is the story of a great soldier, Macbeth, who is told by three witches that he will one day be the King of Scotland. When he tells his wife this news, she becomes power hungry. She decides that they should fulfil the prophesy immediately and murder the present king while he is staying at their castle.

Development

1 On your own, read the following extract from Act I, Scene 7, in which Lady Macbeth is trying to persuade Macbeth to kill Duncan, King of Scotland.

LADY MACBETH	We fail?
	But screw your courage to the sticking-place,
	And we'll not fail. When Duncan is asleep —
	Whereto the rather shall his day's hard journey
	Soundly invite him — his two chamberlains
	Will I with wine and wassail so convince,
	That memory, the warder of the brain,
	Shall be a fume, and the receipt of reason
	A limbeck only: when in swinish sleep
	Their drenched natures lies as in a death,
	What cannot you and I perform upon
	Th'unguarded Duncan, what not put upon
	His spongy officers, who shall bear the guilt
	Of our great quell?
MACBETH	Bring forth men-children only;
	For thy undaunted mettle should compose
	Nothing but males. Will it not be received,
	When we have marked with blood those sleepy two
	Of his own chamber, and used their very daggers,
	That they have done't?
LADY MACBETH	Who dares receive it other,
	As we shall make our griefs and clamor roar
	Upon his death?
MACBETH	I am settled, and bend up
	Each corporal agent to this terrible feat.
	Away, and mock the time with fairest show:
	False face must hide what the false heart doth know.

2 With a partner, each take a part and read the extract again, aloud.

3 Decide between you what Lady Macbeth, in her first lines of dialogue, says she is going to do to Duncan's guards to make Macbeth's task easier.

4 Lady Macbeth's courage and ambition encourage Macbeth to further develop the plan concerning the guards. What does he say he will do?

5 Join another pair and share your ideas between the four of you. Find four adjectives to describe each of the two characters. What are their differences?

6 Staying in your group of four, each pair in turn reads the lines of dialogue again, with the other pair as the audience. This time try to make more sense of the language, using the ideas you have discussed.

7 The audience pair must evaluate how clearly the lines can be understood and how effectively the roles of the two characters are portrayed. Give each actor a mark out of five, with five being the highest mark.

Review

● As a whole class, discuss whether Shakespeare's language was easier or harder to understand than you thought it would be.
● Do a hand count survey of how many of you would like to find out what happened next in the play.

The Demon Headmaster

Aims

- To work in a group to present both scripted and unscripted pieces which maintain the attention of the audience.
- To interpret action, character and events from a scene of the play *The Demon Headmaster*.
- To reflect on your work and that of others.

Starter session

- Brainstorm *The Demon Headmaster*.
- Have you read the novel, or seen the play or TV programme?
- Who are the characters?
- What happens?
- If you have not heard of *The Demon Headmaster*, what does the title suggest to you?

Introduction

Gillian Cross wrote the novel *The Demon Headmaster*, which has since been adapted for both stage and television. The scene you will work on is orphan Dinah's first day at her new school.

KEY WORDS

Cross-cutting is when you stop the action and move back and forward across scenes.

Development

Complete activities A and B.

1 Read the scene from *The Demon Headmaster* in pairs.

Scene 5	*The Head's Office.* **Dawn** *and* **Darryl** *exit, as the* **Head** *enters, wearing sunglasses.* **Sarah** *and* **Simon** *knock at the door.*
HEAD	Enter.
	Sarah *and* **Simon** *take* **Dinah** *in.*
HEAD	Whoever can keep order can rule the world.
SARAH AND SIMON	*(Coming to attention)* Sir!
HEAD	Is this the new girl?
DINAH	I'm Dinah Glass and I…
HEAD	Please do not speak until asked. (To Prefects) You may go.
	Simon *and* **Sarah** *exit.*
	Sit down.
	Dinah *sits down.*
HEAD	I'm going to give you a test all new pupils do.
DINAH	Haven't you got a report from my old school?
HEAD	Other people's reports are no use to me. Please just do as you are told. Spell 'onomatopoeia'.
DINAH	*(Pretends to find this difficult)* Er … er … n …
HEAD	Quickly!
DINAH	*(Flustered)* O…n…o…m…a…t…o…p…o…e…i…a.
HEAD	Correct (To himself) Interesting… What are seventeen 34s? Work it out in your head, please.
DINAH	Erm …
HEAD	Quickly!
DINAH	Five hundred and seventy-eight.
HEAD	Correct. (To himself) Very interesting … What's the chemical formula for sulphuric acid? Quick.
DINAH	H_2SO … (Very deliberately) 5.
HEAD	Incorrect. H_2SO_4. You're an intelligent girl.
	Dinah *looks worried.*
	But careless.
	She relaxes.
	I wonder if … It doesn't matter. We'll find out everything about you in due course. Now you must be feeling tired, Dinah.
DINAH	No.
HEAD	I think you are. (He takes off his sunglasses and looks at her.)
	It's funny you should be so tired this early in the morning.
	Dinah *opens her mouth to contradict him, but can't speak.*
HEAD	You're so tired your head feels heavy, your eyes are starting to close. You're so very tired, very tired …
	Dinah *falls into a hypnotic trance.*

2 Select a short extract from the scene, maximum ten lines (five each). Learn the lines. Give your character an appropriate voice. Now think of an action the character repeats more than once. This action should tell us something about the character.

3 Perform your work to the class.

4 Did the voice and action you selected for your character help maintain the audience's attention?

5 Assess how well you maintained the audience's attention. Give yourself a mark out of five, where five means you totally maintained the attention of the audience.

ACTIVITY **B**

1 Why do people try to control other people? Discuss in groups of four.

2 Make a list of your findings and feed back to the class.

3 In the scene between Dinah and the headmaster, the headmaster dominates the meeting and attempts to control Dinah in a number of ways. Think of times when people have tried to control you.

4 Working in two pairs, create two scenes:
- one in which someone tries to control you for your own good
- one in which someone tries to control you for their own purposes.

5 Now **cross-cut** between the two scenes as you prepare your unscripted performance, then perform your scenes to the class.

Review

- What have you learnt about maintaining the attention of an audience? List five key things that can help you maintain their attention.
- Did your scripted or your unscripted work maintain the audience's attention most? Why do you think this might be?
- Feed back your findings to the class.

Homework

The scene you read cross-cuts to the dining room and then back to the headmaster's office. Write your own version of the second part of the scene after Dinah wakes up. Limit your scene to six lines of dialogue. Aim to keep the audience's attention.

Life Doesn't Frighten Me

Aims

- To use a poem as a starting point to explore situations using the drama technique of **reportage**.
- To reflect on your presentations and those of others.

Starter session

- Writing in groups of four, recollect any stories that you have heard in the media that may have made young children fearful.
- Make a list of five stories. Decide which elements of the story make it frightening for a younger child.
- Feed back your thoughts to the class.

Introduction

Maya Angelou, a Black American writer, educator and performer was born in 1928. She has written many novels and poems that portray childhood. In 'Life Doesn't Frighten Me' she looks at what frightened her as a young child.

KEY WORDS

Reportage is when you use journalistic conventions to interpret and convey events, for example, creating a news report or writing a front page story.

Development

Complete activities A and B.

1 Read the poem aloud individually.

LIFE DOESN'T FRIGHTEN ME

Shadows on the wall
Noises down the hall
Life doesn't frighten me at all
Bad dogs barking load
Big ghost in a cloud
Life doesn't frighten me at all.

Mean old Mother Goose
Lions on the loose
They don't frighten me at all
Dragons breathing flame
On my counterpane
That doesn't frighten me at all.

I go boo
Make them shoo
I make fun
Way them run
I won't cry
So they fly
I just smile
They go wild
Life doesn't frighten me at all.

Tough guys in a fight
All alone at night
Life doesn't frighten me at all.
Panthers in the park

Strangers in the dark
No, they don't frighten me at all.
That new classroom where
Boys all pull my hair
(Kissy little girls
With their hair in curls)
They don't frighten me at all.

Don't show me frogs and snakes
And listen for my scream,
If I'm afraid at all
It's only in my dreams.

I've got a magic charm
That I keep up my sleeve,
I can walk the ocean floor
And never have to breathe.

Life doesn't frighten me at all
Not at all
Not at all
Life doesn't frighten me at all.

by Maya Angelou

2 What are the girl's fears? In pairs, make a list.

3 Now decide which fears are real and which are imagined.

4 Do you think the girl is really frightened or not? Look for clues in the poem that will support your view.

5 Is she giving in to her fears or is she resisting them? Look for clues in the poem again.

6 Feed back your thoughts to the class.

1 In pairs, create a short scene in which one of the girl's fears comes true. Start and end with a still image.

2 Join pairs to make a four and show your piece to the other pair.

3 Observe the scene in role as a reporter for a television news programme. What is there in the scene that you think your audience might be interested in?

4 Now use the drama technique of reportage to interpret the event. Create a news report on the scene you have observed. You may tell the story directly to camera or interview eye witnesses or the people involved. As you create your news report think about your own experience as a consumer of news. Try to make your report as authentic as possible.

5 Now present the scene of the event (pair A) followed by the created news report (pair B) to the class.

Review

- As you watch the work consider:
  - How true to the event is the report?
  - What has the reporter selected as the most important part of the story?
  - Do you think the people involved in the event would be happy with the way it has been reported?
- Feed back your thoughts and findings to the class.

Homework

Write a headline and story for the front page of a newspaper. Decide which was the most interesting of the 'fear' scenes from the lesson and write your report on this. Limit your story to 250 words.

Nooligan

Aims

- To explore in role the impact that relationships have on character.
- To collaborate with others to create a dramatic performance based around the character Nooligan from a poem by Roger McGough.

Starter session

- Think of a negative word or phrase that describes a young person who behaves badly, e.g. hooligan, yob, slob.
- Now change the first letter of the word to create a new word – aim to make the new word funny rather than unpleasant.
- Now share your words with the class.

Introduction

Roger McGough's poem 'Nooligan' comes from a collection of poems called *You At The Back*. As you read the poem, ask yourself why this is a good title for the collection. You will be using the poem's central character as a starting point for your own creative drama work.

Development

1 Read the poem 'Nooligan'.

2 Individually, take it in turns to walk around the space in the way you think Nooligan would walk.

3 Now use your face to create an expression that you think 'Nooligan' might make.

4 In pairs, create three still images that show Nooligan in the following situations:
   – With friends
   – With teachers
   – With family at home

5 In groups of four, develop these still pictures into thirty-second scenes. Be clear about your dramatic intentions: What do you want to say about Nooligan?

6 As you watch the scenes think, 'Which character has the highest and lowest **status** in the scene and how do we know this?'.

7 In groups of four or five, discuss what image Nooligan is trying to convey.

8 How successful is Nooligan in conveying this image?

9 One person from each group feeds back the group's findings to the class.

NOOLIGAN

I'm a nooligan
don't give a toss
in our class
I'm the boss
(well, one of them)

I'm a nooligan
got a nard 'ead
step out of line
and youre dead
(well, bleedin)

I'm a nooligan
I spray me name
all over town
footballs me game
(well, watchin)

I'm a nooligan
violence is fun
gonna be a nassassin
or a nired gun
(well, a soldier)

by Roger McGough

KEY WORDS

Status is the position of power between characters.

43

1 Now imagine that Nooligan has survived adolescence and grown into an adult. Do you think he will have changed at all? Create a series of improvisations that show what Nooligan would be like if he were to become:

– a teacher
– a football referee
– a doctor
– a supermarket manager
– select your own job for Nooligan.

Limit each scene to 30 seconds. Work in groups of four and cross-cut the short scenes together.

2 Present your scenes to the group. Audience: as you watch the work decide if this transformation into adulthood is believable.

3 Audience: feed back your responses to the group.

4 Develop, in groups of four, a piece of drama that shows Nooligan the Teenager and Nooligan the Adult. If his character has changed as he gets older include in your drama what happened to him to make him change.

Review

● In your groups of four, discuss what makes Nooligan the way he is. Think back to the scenes you have created and observed for ideas. Think of three things Nooligan or others could do to help Nooligan be a good citizen.
● Report your findings back to the class.

Homework

Writing in role as Nooligan's mum or dad, write a letter to a magazine's problem page asking for advice on what to do with your son. Use ideas from the lesson to stimulate your writing.

Children in conflict

Aims

- To work in role to explore the issue of children in conflict.
- To create a number of roles and aim to **sustain** them in your performance work.

Starter session

- Working on your own, think of a great line to start an argument with:
  - a classmate
  - a parent
  - a teacher
  - a police officer.
- Take it in turns to speak out your first lines.

Introduction

Conflicts rage around the world and, in the midst of violence and war, families and children go about their daily routines. The image of 'A child in Time' was published in *The Guardian* newspaper in 2001. The photograph was taken in Northern Ireland. You will be using this image as a starting point for your own creative drama work.

KEY WORDS

Hot seating is when a character or person in role sits in the hot seat and questions are fired at them. They must respond in role. It is used for deepening the understanding of the role.

Open questions are questions that you cannot answer 'Yes' or 'No' to. They force the answerer to give a more detailed response.

Closed questions are questions that you answer 'Yes' or 'No' to.

Sustain is when you maintain or remain in a role.

Development

Look at the image from the newspaper and then complete activities A and B.

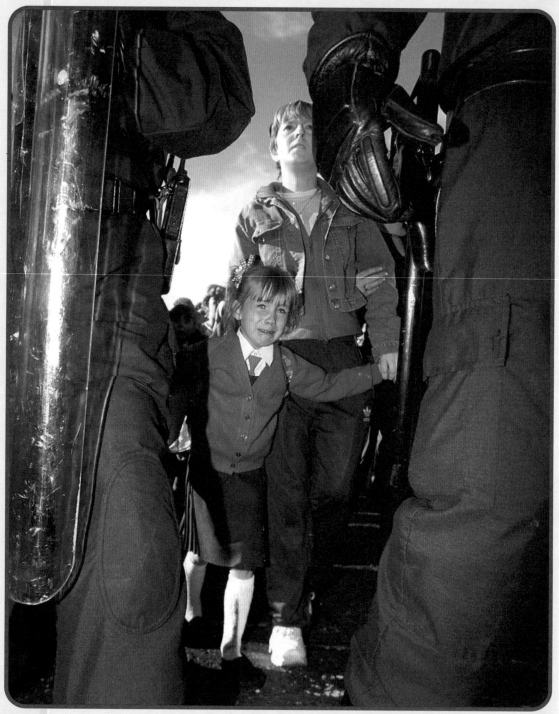

'A Child in Time', *The Guardian*, 7 September 2001

1 In pairs, make a list of the characters that could be in this drama – those in the photograph and possibly others who are not seen.

2 In pairs, create a role-play between the characters with the guns and the woman who is with the child.

3 Watch some of the role-plays and choose an interesting character to **hot seat**.

4 As a whole group, use hot seating to develop a more rounded understanding of the character you are playing – this will help you sustain your character.

5 Think of a question to fire at the character in the hot seat. **Open questions** are better than **closed questions**. When you are in the hot seat you have to answer the questions in role and remember to sustain your character.

6 Now, in pairs, collaborate in writing a short script for the characters you have created in your role-play work. Write five lines for each character. You might want to refer back to the 'argument' first lines from the starter activity.

 ACTIVITY **B**

1 Individually, create a narration for the little girl in the picture. You should speak in role as the little girl and tell the story from her view point.

2 Listen to some other people's narrations.

3 Now, working in groups of three or four, combine the role-plays and the narration to create a dramatic presentation.

4 Present your work to the class.

Review

- The image appeared with the caption 'Why it takes the image of a child to wake the world.' What effect has the image had on you?
- How effectively have you developed this in your drama work?
- Discuss these questions in your groups and feed back your findings to the class.

Homework

Research a current area of conflict in which children are involved and write an imaginary account of a child's day in a conflict zone.

Blood Brothers

Aims

- To develop some techniques to help you create and sustain a role.
- To reflect on your work in role and identify ways of improving it.

Starter session

- Think of a place your parents do not allow you to go. In role as mum or dad, speak aloud their warnings to you. Take it in turns to speak out the warnings around the class.
- As a whole class discuss:
  - Does it make you want to go there more?
  - What are your parents' reasons for the warnings?

Introduction

Blood Brothers has been described as a Liverpudlian *West Side Story*. Mickey and Edward are twins who are separated at birth when their mother, Mrs Johnson, cannot afford to keep them both. Edward is secretly given away to wealthy Mrs Lyons. The boys meet in the extract below and become friends, ignorant of their true relationship.

Development

Complete activities A and B.

ACTIVITY **A**

1 In pairs, read the extract from *Blood Brothers*, one of you taking the part of Mickey and the other playing Edward.

EDWARD: Hello.
MICKEY: (*suspiciously*) Hello.
EDWARD: I've seen you before.
MICKEY: Where?
EDWARD: You were playing with some other boys near my house.
MICKEY: Do you live up in the park?
EDWARD: Yes. Are you going to come and play up there again?
MICKEY: No. I would but I'm not allowed.
EDWARD: Why?
MICKEY: 'Cos me mam says.
EDWARD: Well, my mummy doesn't allow me to play down here actually.
MICKEY: 'Gis a sweet.
EDWARD: All right. (*He offers a bag from his pocket.*)
MICKEY: (*shocked*) What?
EDWARD: Here.
MICKEY: (*trying to work out the catch, suspiciously taking one*)
        Can I have another one? For our Sammy?
EDWARD: Yes, of course. Take as many as you want.
MICKEY: (*taking a handful*): Are you soft?
EDWARD: I don't think so?
MICKEY: Round here if y' ask for a sweet, y' have to ask about, about twenty
        million times. An' y' know what?
EDWARD: (*sitting beside MICKEY*) What?
MICKEY: They still don't bleedin' give y' one. Sometimes our Sammy does
        but y' have to be dead careful if our Sammy gives y' a sweet.
EDWARD: Why?
MICKEY: 'Cos if our Sammy gives y' a sweet he's usually weed on it first.
EDWARD: (*exploding in giggles*): Oh that sounds like super fun.
MICKEY: It is. If y' our Sammy.
EDWARD: Do you want to come and play?

2 Now swap roles and read the extract again.

3 Look carefully at the language used by the characters. In what ways are they different? List three ways in which they are different and link each observation to a piece of evidence in the extract. Feed back your findings to the class.

4 Read the extract again in your pair. Concentrate on how you think the two characters will sound. Think about accent and how the characters shorten words.

5 Now do the scene as a mime. How do you think the two characters will stand, move, gesture? Share your mimed scene with another pair. Can they spot the difference and identify the two characters from your movements?

6 Consider how the two boys would look. What costumes would you put them in and how would they be different? Feed back your findings to the class.

KEY WORDS

Freeze-frame is another name for still image.

ACTIVITY **B**

1 You have developed some techniques to help you create the characters of Mickey and Edward. Can you identify them?

2 At the end of the extract Edward suggests that the boys play together. Create, in pairs, an improvised scene of the boys at play. What do you think they might get up to? Use the voice and movement work you did on the characters earlier to support your role-play. Aim to sustain your work in role. Start and end with a **freeze-frame**. Do not do anything the boys would not do between the two freezes. Set your scene in a place you are forbidden to go. Think back to the starter activity.

3 Perform your improvisations for the class.

Review

Observe other people's improvisations. How well have they sustained their roles? Give them a mark out of five, with five indicating that they fully sustained their roles.

Homework

Use a search engine to research *Blood Brothers* on the Internet to find some production photographs of the play. Are Edward and Mickey what you expected?

Choose me!

Aims

- To read and respond through your drama work to the poem 'Tich Miller' by Wendy Cope.
- To explore and develop in role the ideas, issues and relationships in the poem.

Starter session

- 'I was left out!' Think for a moment about a time when you felt left out in some way. It could be in the playground, at home, in a lesson, with friends, in a club or on the sports field.
- Take turns round the class to speak out your thoughts: 'I was left out when ...' (finish the sentence).
- Discuss, in groups of three, what it feels like to be left out. Feed back your findings to the class.

Introduction

In 'Tich Miller', Wendy Cope deals with issues and relationships you may have encountered in your own experience of childhood. In your drama work you will be using the poem as a starting point for exploring and developing your own ideas and communicating them to others.

Development

Complete activities A and B.

1 In groups of four, make a list of ten things you look for in a friend. Put your list aside and keep it for later.

2 Read the poem 'Tich Miller' silently to yourself.

3 Now read it aloud in your group of four, taking it in turns to read a sentence.

4 Make a list of five words that you think would describe Tich.

5 Create a **role-on–the-wall**. Draw an outline of Tich on the board (or a large sheet of paper).

6 A spokesperson for each group can offer words to add to the picture. Write these words inside the picture.

TICH MILLER

Tich Miller wore glasses
with elastoplast pink frames
and had one foot three sizes larger than the other.

When they picked teams for outdoor games
she and I were always the last two
left standing by the wire-mesh fence.

We avoided one another's eyes,
Stooping, perhaps, to re-tie a shoelace,
Or affecting interest in the flight

of some fortunate bird, and pretending
not to hear the urgent conference:
'Have Tubby!' 'No, no, have Tich!'

Usually they chose me, the lesser dud,
And she lolloped, unselected,
to the back of the other team.

At eleven we went to different schools.
In time I learned to get my own back,
sneering at hockey-players who couldn't spell.

Tich died when she was twelve.

by Wendy Cope

KEY WORDS

A **role-on-the-wall** is when a character is recorded in picture form, on the board or a large sheet of paper. Information about the character can be added or deleted as the character develops through the drama.

1 Join with another group of four to make an eight. Create in mime the scene that is described in the poem. The only character that is allowed to speak is Tich. Tich does not actually say anything in the poem so she should speak only her thoughts.

2 View the scenes that have been created and reflect on the role-on-the-wall. Is there anything you want to change?

3 In the poem we discover that Tich died at twelve. If she had not died, what sort of adult character do you think she would have grown into? Refer to the role-on-the-wall and, in pairs, create a new scene that shows the audience Tich Miller as an adult. You will need to decide who the second character is. When working, show how her treatment as a child might affect her behaviour as an adult. Limit your scene to one minute.

4 Perform your work for the class and add to the role-on-the-wall as required.

Review

- Look again at your list of how it feels to be left out (from the starter activity). In groups of four, discuss the consequences of leaving people out. Think of three consequences and feed back your findings to the class.
- Now look at your list of things you look for in a friend. What advice would you give Tich to help her make friends? Think of three things and feed them back to the class.

Far-out folks

Aims

- To develop the dramatic techniques that enable you to create and sustain a role.
- To consider the **drama skills** others use, and how they could extend and develop these skills in their work.

Starter session

- In groups of five, write down a list of skills you use in drama. Think back to other drama lessons or think of plays or films you have seen. What skills are the actors using?
- Report back to the class, and keep your findings as you will be using them later.

Introduction

John Agard, a poet from Guyana, explores the influence that parents' behaviour has on their teenage children in his poem 'Way-Out Mum, Way-Out Dad'. You will be using this as a starting point for your drama work.

Development

1 Read the poem silently to yourself.

WAY-OUT MUM
WAY-OUT DAD

Mum dyes her hair incandescent green
and paints her nails
a shade of midnight blue.

Dad wears a ponytail, listens to Cream
and goes on about a book
called The Tao Of Pooh.

What do you do when your parents are so liberal
they pinch your rap and heavy metal
and don't mind a nosering or tattoo?

It embarrasses me to tell,
but when their bedroom gives off that incense smell,
I know – I just know – they're smooching
and carrying on to a small Tibetan bell.

Oh what do you do with a mum and dad
who're so cool, streetwise and hip to the scene,
they make me feel like a has-been
and I'm only fourteen.

They've given me nothing
against which I can rebel.
Just to annoy them I'll grow up
sweet and straight as an angel.

by John Agard

2 Now read it aloud, taking turns around the class, doing a line each.
   Read it a couple of times.

3 The poem's comedy relies on the **role reversal** of its characters. Can you
   think of any examples of role reversal being used in plays, films or
   television programmes?

4 In groups of four, decide whether you think having 'way-out' parents is a
   good thing or a bad thing. Think of reasons to justify your decision.

5 In your groups create two scenes:
   – One that shows a conventional parent–teenager relationship
   – One that shows a 'way-out' or liberal parent–teenager relationship.

6 Use the decision you made earlier to decide on your group's **dramatic intentions**. Devise and rehearse your pieces.

7 Connect the two scenes into one performance. Consider using freeze frame, **montage** or thought tracking to connect the two scenes.

8 Reflect on your work in progress; ask yourselves if you are communicating your dramatic intentions.

KEY WORDS

Drama skills are the techniques you can develop to increase your ability to convey ideas to an audience. They include: voice, movement, gesture, facial expression, pace, spacing levels and status.

Dramatic intentions are what you intend the audience to think or feel or consider on seeing your drama.

Montage is when you create a series of images or scenes that contrast, challenge and encourage an audience to take a new look at the subject.

Role reversal is when you swap roles to see the situation from another point of view.

Review

- Look at the lists of skills you identified in the starter activity. How many of these have you used in your improvised plays? As you watch other groups perform their work, consider the drama skills they have used and how they could extend and develop these skills in their work.
- How have the groups used voice, movement, gesture, facial expression, timing, pace, spacing, levels and status to convey their ideas in the performance?
- Report back to the groups that have shown their work.

Homework
Write an account of your improvisation; evaluate how effectively you used your drama skills to convey your ideas to the audience.

All the world's a stage

Aims

- To refine your interpretation of a well known extract from *As You Like It* by William Shakespeare, and to use it as a starting point for your own drama work.
- To reflect on your own drama work and developing it using drama techniques.

Starter session

- How many important stages are there in life? How do you know when you get there? Discuss this in groups of four and make a list of your findings.
- Feed back your findings to the class.

Introduction

In Shakespeare's play *As You Like It*, the duke has been banished by his younger brother and is living in the forest. In the extract starting 'All the world's a stage', the duke's friend, Jaques, speaks his thoughts to him. In the speech, Shakespeare divides life into seven ages – identify these as you read the extract.

Development

Complete activities A, B and C.

1 In your groups of four, read the extract aloud. Take it in turns to read two lines at a time.

All the world's a stage,
And all the men and women merely players:
They have their exits and their entrances;
And one man in his time plays many parts,
His acts being seven ages. At first the infant,
Mewling and puking in the nurse's arms.
And then the whining school-boy, with his satchel
And shining morning face, creeping like snail
Unwillingly to school. And then the lover,
Sighing like furnace, with a woeful ballad
Made to his mistress' eyebrow. Then a soldier,
Full of strange oaths and bearded like the pard,
Jealous in honour, sudden and quick in quarrel,
Seeking the bubble reputation
Even in the cannon's mouth. And then the justice,
In fair round belly with good capon lined,
With eyes severe and beard of formal cut,
Full of wise saws and modern instances;
And so he plays his part. The sixth age shifts
Into the lean and slipper'd pantaloon,
With spectacles on nose and pouch on side,
His youthful hose, well saved, a world too wide
For his shrunk shank; and his big manly voice,
Turning again toward childish treble, pipes
And whistles in his sound. Last scene of all,
That ends this strange eventful history,
Is second childishness and mere oblivion,
Sans teeth, sans eyes, sans taste, sans everything.

As You Like It by *William Shakespeare, Act 2, Scene 7*

2 For each of the seven ages create a still image that identifies a stage of life. Give each still image a caption (not more than three words) taken from the text of the extract.

3 Present your still images and captions to the class.

1 Do you think that age determines the way people behave? Discuss this in pairs. Do people ever behave in unexpected ways that might be more appropriate to other stages of life? Can you recall any experience of this happening?

2 In pairs, create the following short scenes (one minute maximum) in which the expected behaviour of the characters is reversed:
   – Child and parent: parent does not want to eat their meal.
   – Teenager and parent: parent is late back from a party.
   – Parent and grandparent: grandparent has a new girlfriend/boyfriend.
   – Grandparent and teenager: grandparent needs advice.

3 Show a selection of your improvisations to the class.

4 In pairs, discuss the effect that reversing the expected behaviour of the characters had on the audience.

1 In *As You Like It*, Jaques sees life as an inevitable journey from birth to death. He is a realist, or possibly even a pessimist. Take a different view to Jaques. What would be the ideal seven ages of man or woman?

2 Work in groups of four to create seven thirty-second scenes, each with a title of not more than three words. This montage of scenes should communicate your 'ideal' seven ages. Rehearse and present them.

Review

● What are the main differences between the still images you made in Activity A and the seven scenes you presented in Activity C?
● In what ways are they similar?
● Do you think people should conform to Jaques' seven ages, or should they do their own thing?

Homework
Write an account of your contribution to the presentations you have made this lesson. What do you think of the ideas that have been explored in the lesson?

Lyra's dilemma

Aims

- To explore the **dilemma** in which Lyra finds herself, through the use of role-play and thought tunnel techniques.
- To work with others to present and evaluate a piece of unscripted drama.

Starter session

- In groups of three or four, discuss situations in which you have been unable to own up to something for fear of getting into trouble (e.g. forgetting to close the hamster cage door, resulting in the cat eating the hamster!).
- Select the most interesting situation and describe it to the rest of the class.

Introduction

In this unit you will be working on an extract from Philip Pullman's novel *Northern Lights*, the first book of his trilogy. Some of you may have read this exciting story and your knowledge of the narrative and characters will be useful.

KEY WORDS

A **dilemma** is a problem with two possible outcomes.

Development

1 In the following extract, Lyra, a determined and inquisitive girl, finds herself in a dilemma. Read the text carefully on your own to work out what is happening in the scene.

Note that Pantalaimon is Lyra's guardian spirit (dæmon), in the form of a moth.

From her not-much-of-a-hiding place Lyra watched as the Master went to a large oak wardrobe in the corner of the room, took his gown from a hanger, and pulled it laboriously on. The Master had been a powerful man, but he was well over seventy now, and his movements were stiff and slow. The Master's dæmon had the form of a raven, and as soon as his robe was on, she jumped down from the wardrobe and settled in her accustomed place on his right shoulder.

Lyra could feel Pantalaimon bristling with anxiety, though he made no sound. For herself, she was pleasantly excited. The visitor mentioned by the Master, Lord Asriel, was her uncle, a man whom she admired and feared greatly. He was said to be involved in high politics, in secret exploration, in distant warfare, and she never knew when he was going to appear. He was fierce: if he caught her in here she'd be severely punished, but she could put up with that.

What she saw next, however, changed things completely.

The Master took from his pocket a folded paper and laid it on the table. He took the stopper out of the mouth of a decanter containing a rich golden wine, unfolded the paper, and poured a thin stream of white powder into the decanter before crumpling the paper and throwing it into the fire. Then he took a pencil from his pocket and stirred the wine until the powder had dissolved, and replaced the stopper.

His dæmon gave a soft brief squawk. The Master replied in an undertone, and looked around with his hooded, clouded eyes before leaving through the door he'd come in by.

2 In pairs, describe the scene in your own words, taking it in turns to give one sentence at a time.

3 Lyra knows that very soon her uncle, Lord Asriel, will enter the room. What is Lyra's dilemma? In your pair, discuss this and feed back to the class.

4 As a whole class, create a thought tunnel for Lyra before the entrance of her uncle.

5 In pairs, role-play a scene in which Lyra and Pantalaimon decide what to do. (Pantalaimon is the voice of caution.) Use only four lines of dialogue each.

6 Join another pair and present your scene to each other. Evaluate the work and decide which scene is the most interesting.

7 In your group of four, now devise the scene that takes place when Lord Asriel and his dæmon, a snow leopard, find Lyra and Pantalaimon in the forbidden room.

8 Before you begin, think carefully about how you will play the dæmons. Remember that they are not comic characters.

9 Start and end the scene with a still image.

10 Present your improvisations to the rest of the class.

Review

As a member of the audience, consider how effectively the characters show the sense of urgency in the situation, and how well the actors have managed to tackle the difficult characterisations of the dæmons.

Black Harvest

Aims

- To use the play *Black Harvest* to help you develop the dramatic techniques to create various roles and to explore the issue of famine.
- To work with others to present a dramatic performance.

Starter session

- In groups of four, brainstorm the word 'famine'. What does it mean? Why do famines occur? Can you think of any recent examples?
- Feed back your ideas to the rest of the class.

Introduction

As a starting point for your drama work, you will be using an extract from the play *Black Harvest* by Nigel Gray. Colin, his sister Prill and their cousin Oliver are holidaying in a new cottage on the west coast of Ireland, along with their mother and baby sister Alison.

Soon after their arrival, some strange happenings occur in and around the cottage. It seems that Oliver's archaeological dig in the garden has unearthed some ghosts from the past – the famine and the Morissey family.

Development

1 In a group of four, read aloud the following extract in which the local priest tells the three children about the history of the village during the Irish Potato Famine of the 1840s.

FATHER HAGAN	It's hard to believe some of the tales about the famine years, but what happened to the Morrissey's wasn't unusual.
PRILL	What **did** happen to them?
FATHER HAGAN	Well, at that time, they would have worked as labourers on the landlord's land — land which had once been their own. They would have been paid, of course, but their earnings were small and had to be repaid to the landlord as rent for their cottage and for the little plot of land on which they grew potatoes.
OLIVER	The potatoes they grew were all the poor had to live on.
FATHER HAGAN	In better years they might have had a few hens or a pig.
OLIVER	The famine years were good years, weren't they, for all crops except potatoes?
FATHER HAGAN	Yes indeed. Wet springs and hot summers — very much like this year, in fact — ideal conditions for potato blight. The English landlords grew rich exporting food under armed guard while the poor died of starvation. People killed off their dogs and ate them. Some people ate rats.
OLIVER	Some even fed on the bodies of those that had died. It was a kind of cannibalism.
FATHER HAGAN	Possibly, possibly. *He gives **Oliver** a 'look'.* But I don't think there was a lot of that.
COLIN	There couldn't have been much meat on the bodies if they'd died of starvation.
FATHER HAGAN	Starvation and disease. When people are seriously malnourished they are at the mercy of every illness, and epidemics spread like wildfire.
OLIVER	There were so many bodies, lots remained unburied, or were thrown into great pits — mass graves — and covered with lime.
FATHER HAGAN	That's quite right Oliver. And they say the children came to look like monkeys, wizened and covered with hair; and they lost their powers of speech. In the end they could only open and close their mouths but no sound came through. The potato fields turned black with the blight — they looked as though fire had passed over them. And during those hot summers, the awful stench of rotting potatoes hung over everything. The entire potato harvest was destroyed almost overnight, for several years running.

2 In your group, discuss what you have learnt from the extract about the famine and what happened to the starving people. Recount two facts each.

3 Using this information, improvise a scene in which a reporter from *The Illustrated London News* arrives at the Morrisey's cottage in 1847 to interview them about the potato blight situation. Begin and end your work with a still image.

4 Present these scenes to the whole class. As an audience, evaluate:
  – How effectively the actors showed the desperate plight of the family
  – How accurately they presented all the facts described in the scene above

5 Working as a whole class, choose one person to play the part of the reporter.

6 Decide on a name for him (it would probably have been a man at this time) and then hot seat him. Ask him questions about his meeting with the Morrisey family and how he felt about their situation.

7 Working in pairs, use the information gained from the hot seating exercise to improvise a scene between the reporter and the Morrisey's English Landlord when they meet in the local pub.

Review

● As a class, remind yourselves of what you have learnt about the Famine in Ireland in the 1840s. How do you feel about what happened?
● Evaluate your own contribution to the lesson and how well you think you played the various roles within the scenes. Give yourself a mark out of five.

Bullets at the back door

Aims

- To work in role to explore the experience of living in a war zone.
- To collaborate in devising, presenting and evaluating a dramatic performance.

Starter session

- In pairs, write one sentence describing what you think it is like to live in a country that is at war.
- Each pair reads out their idea to the class.
- Discuss the overall picture you have built up.

Introduction

Zlata Filipovic, aged 11, wrote a diary of her life in Sarajevo before and during the war in Bosnia. Her diary was published in France and it showed us how quickly the world she had known fell apart. You will be using extracts from her diary as starting points for your own creative work.

Development

1 Read the following extract on your own

Tuesday, 10 September 1991

The week was spent getting my books and school supplies, describing how we spent our holidays on the seaside, in the mountains, in the countryside and abroad. We all went somewhere and we all have so much to tell one another.

2 In groups of four, produce a still image of Zlata meeting up with her friends after the summer holiday.

3 Now read the following extract on your own.

Sunday, 5 April 1992

Dear Mimmy,
I'm trying to concentrate so I can do my homework (reading), but I simply can't. Something is going on in town. You can hear gunfire from the hills. Columns of people are spreading out from Dobrinja. They're trying to stop something, but they themselves don't know what. You can simply feel that something is coming, something very bad ... The radio keeps playing the same song: 'Sarajevo, My Love'. That's all very nice, but my stomach is still in knots and I can't concentrate on my homework any more.
     Mimmy, I'm afraid of WAR!!!
Zlata

4 In the same groups of four, produce a still image representing what is happening in the extract.

5 Now put your two still images together, one after the other.

6 Decide on a caption for each one.

7 Now read the final extract at the end of Zlata's diary.

Sunday, 17 October 1993

Dear Mimmy,
Yesterday our 'friends in the hills' reminded us of their presence and that they are now in control and can kill, wound, destroy ...
    We went down into the cellar. Into the cold, dark, stupid cellar which I hate. We were there for hours and hours. They kept pounding away. All the neighbours were with us.
    ... sub-humans want to destroy us. Why? I keep asking myself, why? We haven't done anything. We're innocent. But helpless!
Zlata

8 In your group, produce a third still image from the above ideas. Give it a caption.

9 Now put all three pieces together. This time include one line of dialogue from each character for each image.

Review

● Each group presents their devised piece of work to the class.
● Evaluate how effectively each group has shown the transformation in Zlata's life.

Loser

Aims

- To explore and develop ideas and relationships through your work in role, using the issue of addiction.

Starter session

- In groups of six, brainstorm the word 'addiction'. A dictionary definition of the word is: 'the condition of being abnormally dependent on some habit'.
- Think of as many different types of addiction as you can.
- Now consider what causes people to become addicts of a particular habit.
- Feed back your ideas to the rest of the class.

Introduction

As a starting point for your drama work, you will be using an extract from Charles Dickens' novel *The Old Curiosity Shop*. Dickens (1812–70) is one of the most famous English novelists of all time. He is popular for his memorable characters and his portrayal of the social evils of Victorian England.

The tragic heroine of this novel is orphan Little Nell, who lives with her grandfather. He becomes a compulsive gambler because he wants to win money to give her a better life. He loses everything and the two are forced to run away from London to start a new life in the country. On their travels, however, it soon becomes clear to Little Nell that his passion for gambling has not left him.

Development

Complete activities A and B.

1 On your own, read the following extract in which the grandfather is tempted into a game of cards with the 'cardsharpers', Isaac List and

'The gentleman has thought better of it, and isn't coming,' said Isaac, making as though he would rise from the table. 'I'm sorry the gentleman's daunted—nothing venture, nothing have—but the gentleman knows best.'

'Why I am ready. You have all been slow but me,' said the old man. 'I wonder who is more anxious to begin than I.'

As he spoke he drew a chair to the table; and the other three closing round it at the same time, the game commenced.

The child sat by, and watched its progress with a troubled mind. Regardless of the run of luck, and mindful only of the desperate passion which had its hold upon her grandfather, losses and gains were to her alike. Exulting in some brief triumph, or cast down by a defeat, there he sat so wild and restless, so feverishly and intensely anxious, so terribly eager, so ravenous for the paltry stakes, that she could have almost better borne to see him dead. And yet she was the innocent cause of all this torture, and he, gambling with such a savage thirst for gain as the most insatiable gambler never felt, had not one selfish thought!

2 With a partner discuss:
  – The character of the old man described in the scene. Which adjectives and adverbs are used to describe how he feels about the card game?
  – Little Nell's reaction to his decision to join the gamblers.

3 In your pair, create a still image of these two characters that clearly illustrates their difference of feeling towards the game.

4 Introduce one line of thought tracking for each character.

5 Present some of these to the rest of the class. As an audience, consider how effectively the actors have captured the atmosphere of the scene.

1 Join another pair to make a group of four. Think back to the starter activity and choose an addictive habit on which to base your own drama work.

2 Devise a short scene which must include the following:
 – A character being tempted into the addictive behaviour
 – A friend trying to persuade them against it
 – No more than eight lines of dialogue

3 Give your devised piece a title.

4 Present your work to the class.

Review

As a class, **debate** the following: 'People who become addicts are selfish'.

KEY WORDS

When you **debate** you have a formal argument in which the participants argue a point of view which may or may not be their own.

Dad's advice

Aims

- To create and sustain a variety of roles in your drama work and explore the issue of 'parental advice'.

Starter session

Think for thirty seconds, 'What advice do I get from the adult who looks after me?' Now quickly go round the class speaking out the advice, as if you were a parent.

Introduction

William Shakespeare wrote the following lines for the character of Polonius in his play Hamlet. Polonius is speaking to his son, Laertes, who is setting off to make his own way in the world.

KEY WORDS

An **aside** is when an actor speaks in character directly to the audience without the other characters hearing.

Development

Complete activities A and B.

1 Read the passage to yourself. As you read the passage, think, 'Have I heard any of this advice before?'.

POLONIUS: There – my blessing with thee!
And these few precepts in thy memory
Look thou character. Give thy thoughts no tongue,
Nor any unproportioned thought his act.
Be thou familiar, but by no means vulgar:
Those friends thou hast, and their adoption tried,
Grapple them unto thy soul with hoops of steel,
But do not dull thy palm with entertainment
Of each new-hatched, unfledged courage. Beware
Of entrance to a quarrel, but being in,
Bear't that th' opposed may beware of thee.
Give every man thy ear, but few thy voice,
Take each man's censure, but reserve thy judgment.
Costly thy habit as thy purse can buy,
But not expressed in fancy, rich, not gaudy,
For the apparel oft proclaims the man,
And they in France of the best rank and station
Are of a most select and generous chief in that.
Neither a borrower nor a lender be,
For loan oft loses both itself and friend,
And borrowing dulleth th'edge of husbandry.
This above all: to thine own self be true,
And it must follow, as the night the day,
Thou canst not then be false to any man.
Farewell, my blessing season this in thee!
LAERTES: Most humbly do I take my leave, my lord.

2 As a whole class, read the passage aloud, taking it in turns to read two lines at a time.

3 In pairs, translate the advice into your own words. Concentrate on what you think are the five most useful pieces of advice that Polonius offers.

4 Select the best piece of advice and, in your own words, give the advice to the class.

5   In pairs, create a scene in which one person plays a parent and the other a teenager who is leaving home. The person playing the parent must speak the words, while the teenager speaks out the thoughts they have about the advice. Imagine the parent cannot hear these thoughts; only the audience can. This is thought tracking. Shakespeare would have called this an **aside**. Now swap roles and repeat the exercise in the other role. As you work, make sure you do not come out of character – sustain your role.

6   Now show the best fifteen to thirty seconds of the role-play to the class.

1   In groups of three to five, create a short play in which you show the consequences of not following a piece of good advice from an adult. Start and end your piece with a still image. In your performance, include a moment when one of the characters speaks their thoughts to the audience (thought tracking/aside).

2   As you watch other groups' plays, ask yourself, 'Do they support the advice or not?'.

Review

- How well did you sustain your character when working in role? Give yourself a mark out of five, where five is the highest mark.
- In pairs, consider how parental advice has changed since Shakespeare's time. Feed back your views to your teacher and the rest of the class.

Homework

- Write a speech that your carer/parent might make to you when you leave home. Before you start writing, do some research; ask them what they think.

Teechers

Aims

- To identify and extend your vocal skills when conveying character.
- To assess the **dramatic impact** of a scene on an audience.
- To write a critical evaluation of a scene in which you have participated.

KEY WORDS

Dramatic impact is the effect a piece of drama has on the audience.

A **round** is when you say or sing lines repeatedly.

Starter session

Think about your school. Imagine that it is a film set and that all the people in it are actors playing the characters. You are auditioning for a part in the film and the director is casting the film based on the following activity.

Walk around the space as:

- the caretaker
- the headteacher
- the maths teacher
- the PE teacher
- the drama teacher
- an angry mum
- a dinner lady
- the school bully
- a swot
- the school inspector.

When you watch other people doing the walks, identify the elements that convey character.

Introduction

John Godber's play *Teechers* is a comedy in which three school leavers do a play about teachers. The three actors play thirty-one characters between them. You will be conveying some of these characters using vocal and movement skills.

Development

1 In groups of three, read aloud the following passage three times as a **round**. The characters of Salty, Gail and Hobby have introduced themselves to the audience and now begin their play.

A sudden burst of music. They become teachers, with briefcases and files, walking about a number of corridors. The lights become brighter.

SALTY	Morning.
GAIL	Morning.
HOBBY	Morning.
SALTY	Morning.
HOBBY	Morning.
GAIL	Morning.
PARRY	Stop running Simon Patterson.
TEACHER A	Morning, Ted.
PARRY	Morning Roy.
TEACHER B	Morning Mr Basford.
ALL	Morning Mrs Parry.
PARRY	Good morning.
WITHAM	You are chewing, girl, spit it out. Not into her hair into the bin…
TEACHER B	I don't call that a straight line, do you, Claire Dickinson? No? Neither do I.
PARRY	I know that was the bell, Simon Patterson. The bell is a signal for me to move and not for anyone else.

2 Keep repeating this until you have learnt the lines.

3 Now think back to the starter activity and add some of these movements to your dialogue to help convey character.

4 Run the dialogue and the movement together and consider the impact you want your sequence to have on an audience. Write down your dramatic intentions.

5 Now write a further fifteen lines of dialogue to follow on from John Godber's lines.

6 Rehearse the full sequence and present your performance to the class.

Review

- In this unit you have worked as actor, writer and, to some extent, director. In discussion in your group, identify your individual contributions. Feed back to the class.
- Give yourself a mark out of five, where five is the highest, on how well you have used your vocal and movement skills to convey character.

Homework

- Write a critical evaluation of the scene you have created in this unit, identifying your personal contribution as writer, director and actor.

The last straw

Aims

- To use a range of drama techniques, including working in role, still image, thought tracking, devising and presenting, to explore the issue of migration in America in the 1930s.
- To convey the **atmosphere** and tension of the scenes you devise, through your characterisations.

Starter session

- As a class, brainstorm what you understand by the words 'migration', the 'Golden West', and 'oppression'.
- Use spider diagrams on three separate sheets of paper to record these ideas and discuss your findings.

Introduction

As a starting point for your work, you will be using an extract from American novelist John Steinbeck's best-known work, *The Grapes of Wrath*. The characters in his novels are often poor and oppressed people, trying to work the land, caught up in a battle for survival against nature or their fellow men. *The Grapes of Wrath* gives a realistic account of the Joad family, from the impoverished Oklahoma dust bowl, migrating to California during the economic depression of the 1930s.

KEY WORDS

Atmosphere is the general feeling created for an audience by the characters.

Development

Complete activities A and B.

 ACTIVITY A

1 Individually read the following extract:

The people came out of their houses and smelled the hot stinging air and covered their noses from it. And the children came out of the houses, but they did not run or shout as they would have done after a rain. Men stood by their fences and looked at the ruined corn, dying fast now, only a little green showing through the film of dust. The men were silent and they did not move often. And the women came out of the houses to stand beside their men – to feel whether this time the men would break. The women studied the men's faces secretly, for the corn could go, as long as something else remained. The children stood near by, drawing figures in the dust with bare toes, and the children sent exploring senses out to see whether men and women would break... After a while the faces of the watching men lost their bemused perplexity and became hard and angry and resistant.

2 In groups of six, discuss the content of the extract. What has taken place and what is happening now?

3 Each group now produce a still image of the scene after the storm, representing the characters of the men, women and children.

4 Introduce thought tracking for each of your characters and present your image to the class. Remember to try to build the tension of the piece. Do not rush your work.

5 Decide which group most effectively captures the atmosphere and tension of the extract. Analyse why.

6 Working in the same group, adopt the characters of the Joad family and discuss the advantages and disadvantages of moving to California to start a new life. Consider the following facts in your drama: it is an extremely long journey, your vehicle is unreliable, petrol is expensive, you have old and young amongst you and you have no proof that there really is housing and jobs in California.

7 Two of the groups present their work to the class.

As an audience, decide whether similar characters in the groups had similar opinions on the move. For which characters would a move be most difficult?

 ACTIVITY **B**

1 Work with a partner. Imagine you are siblings who have been told to leave your home quickly because of a disaster. You are each permitted to take only one possession with you. Explain to each other what you have chosen and why it is so valuable to you.

2 Devise a short scene in which your chosen possessions become a source of comfort to you at a difficult time on your journey to a new home.

Review

- As a class, discuss what kinds of possessions were chosen in Activity B1.
- Discuss the range of emotions you would feel if you had to leave your home, belongings and familiar environment to start a new life.

Homework
- Research the 1930s' American Migration. Find out what happened to many of the families who were forced off their land, and the conditions they lived in when they reached the 'Golden West'.

Lads and lasses

Aims

- To use role-play to explore the issues surrounding gender stereotypes.
- To create characters, conveying action in performing your own plays.

Starter session

- In same-sex pairs, think of a list of five words that describe:
  (a) lads (b) girls.
- Now join up pairs to make same sex fours. Create a one-minute **dramatic sequence** with sound and movement, but no words, which shows how (a) lads (b) girls behave in the playground.
- Groups present their sequences to the class. Are these sequences a fair representation? Discuss this in your group.
- Feed back your views to the class.

KEY WORDS

Dramatic sequence is the group of scenes or events that make up your devised play. It suggests that one thing follows on from another.

Introduction

Andrew Fusek Peters and Polly Peters in *Poems with Attitude* write about real life. In this extract from two connected poems, 'Slugs and snails and puppy dog's tails' and 'Sugar and spice and all things nice', they challenge us to explore the issues surrounding gender.

Development

1 Read the poems on your own.

SLUGS & SNAILS & PUPPY DOGS' TAILS

Lads like football, lads like cars,
Lads like hanging round in bars.
Lads fart to start up conversations
And hang in gangs at railway stations.
Lads show off by acting tough,
And don't know when they've drunk enough.
Lads love Larger with designer labels,
But end up legless under tables.
Lads like playing contact sport,
And wear the socks their mothers bought.
Lads play rugby, lads play pool,
But often don't do well at school.
Lads wear T-shirts when it's chilly
With no idea that they look silly.
Lads can't cook and lads can't sew,
They'd rather sit and watch grass grow.
Lads, you know are king sized rats
However I can tell you that's
A load of crap from where I'm sitting,
'Cos I'm a lad who's into knitting!

SUGAR & SPICE & ALL THINGS NICE

Girls are sugary, girls are spicy,
Girls like trainers that are pricy.
Girls like pink and fluffy stuff,
Girls are sweet and don't act tough.
Girls wear high-rise, platform heels,
Girls theorise on how love feels.
Girls like boys, and girls like dates,
Girls like shopping with their mates.
Girls keep secrets from their mums,
And like to eye up cute boys' bums.
Girls like talk that lays souls bare,
Girls like to style each other's hair.

Girls are friends 'til death do part,
But steal their bloke and you're a tart!
Girls like gossip, girls like bitching,
Snipping friendship's careful stitching.
Girls compare who they have kissed,
Girls can wound without their fist.
Girls read books about romance,
And step round handbags when they dance.
But this girl thinks this list is barmy,
'Cos she's just off to join the army!

2 In pairs, choose one of the poems to respond to.

3 One person plays the character whose voice we hear in the poem; the other plays another character, who disagrees with the views expressed in the poem.

4 Create a role-play in which these characters disagree.

5 Now team up with another pair to make a four. Present your role-plays in turn.

6 Now create a presentation in which you cross-cut between the two role-plays.

7 Decide what statement you want your performance to make. Review your presentation and refine your work to ensure your intentions are clearly communicated to your audience.

8 Present your work to the class.

Review

- As you watch other groups perform, try to work out what statement on the issue the group are making. Feed this back to them.
- In your groups, mark yourselves out of five on how well you conveyed your dramatic intentions.
- What effect did the cross-cutting have on the audience?
- What have you learnt of the issue from the poems and your drama exploration?

Law-breaker

Aims

- To analyse the language, form and dramatic impact of a scene from Sophocles' play *Antigone*.
- To use a range of drama techniques to explore the actions of Antigone and the dilemma of Creon.

Starter session

- Individually, read the following information about Ancient Greek Theatre.

Sophocles' plays were first performed at annual drama competitions in Athens 2500 years ago, in huge open air theatres called amphitheatres, as shown in the picture.

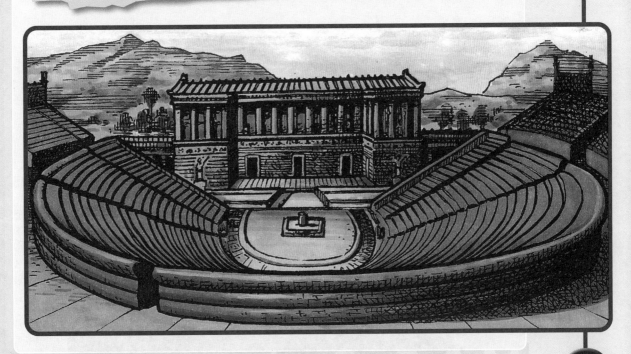

Plays were performed in the daytime to audiences of over 13 000. Actors probably wore little or no makeup. Instead, they carried masks with exaggerated facial expressions. There was little or no scenery.

- Working in pairs, call yourselves A and B then role-play the following scene:
  - A is an actor from Ancient Greece who performs in an Amphitheatre
  - B is a modern-day actor.
- The two of you are having a moan about who has the hardest job!
- Present some of these complaints to the class and analyse the findings.

Introduction

Antigone is a strong-willed young woman whose sense of family loyalty drives her to defy her uncle Creon, the newly crowned King of Thebes. He has decreed that the dead body of his enemy, Antigone's brother Polyneices, be left unburied and eaten by birds of prey. Antigone buries her brother, as the Greeks believed the soul of an unburied body could not be released. Her action is punishable by death.

Development

1 Individually, read the following scene in which Antigone (pronounced Antigony) tries to justify her actions to her uncle.

ANTIGONE: Now you have caught, will you do more than kill me?
CREON: No, nothing more; that is all I could wish.
ANTIGONE: Why then delay? There is nothing that you can say
That I should wish to hear, as nothing I say
Can weigh with you. I have given my brother burial.
What greater honour could I wish? All these
Would say that what I did was honourable,
But fear locks up their lips. To speak and act
Just as he likes is a king's prerogative.
CREON: You are wrong. None of my subjects thinks as you do.
ANTIGONE: Yes, sir, they do; but dare not tell you so.
CREON: And you are not only alone, but unashamed.
ANTIGONE: There is no shame in honouring my brother.

2 In pairs, decide which words and phrases Antigone uses to express and emphasise her defiance of her uncle.

3 Now improvise a scene in which Antigone is telling her more cautious sister Ismene (pronounced Ismenay) why she disobeyed the King and buried their brother. Remember that Creon is a powerful man, keen to assert his rule as the new king, and his words at the end of the above scene are: 'We'll have no woman's law here, while I live.'

4 Present some of these improvisations to the rest of the class.

5 As a class, decide why Antigone's actions have created such a dilemma for Creon. Consider the facts that she is his niece and is engaged to marry his son.

6 Now make a thought tunnel for Creon to walk through. Those down one side express his reasons for not condemning Antigone to death, while those on the other side express his thoughts in favour of such an outcome.

7 In pairs, recreate Sophocles' scene as written. Using what you have learnt about Greek theatre and the characterisations of Antigone and Creon, try to give the scene the dramatic impact it deserves. Remember how strong-willed both these characters are!

Review

- Two groups present their work to the class.
- As an audience, compare the presentations and evaluate how effectively the actors established their roles.
- Evaluate your own work in role by giving yourself a mark out of five, where five is the highest.

No smoke without fire

Aims

- To recognise, evaluate and extend the techniques you have developed through drama.
- To work in role to explore the idea of mutual respect.

Starter session

- Working in pairs, think of an adult for whom you have a great deal of respect. It could be a parent, grandparent or neighbour. Describe your chosen person to your partner and explain why you feel respect for them.
- Now recall a time when you did something that you think upset this person, or that they disapproved of. How did their disapproval make you feel?
- Share some of these moments with the rest of the class.

Introduction

As a starting point for your drama work, you will use an extract from the short story *Smoke*, by Ila Mehta.

Smoke, originally written in Gujarati, is set in a town in India. Dr Shubha lives with her mother-in-law, Ba, following the untimely deaths of both their husbands. Ba is an old lady for whom the beliefs and cultural traditions of Hinduism are very important. Shubha is an educated, modern Indian woman who would like to live a little differently from her mother-in-law, but out of respect does not wish to offend her.

Development

Complete activities A and B.

1 On your own, read the following extract in which Ba and Shubha sit down to share a meal after Ba's return from being away at a family wedding.

Suddenly, Ba's voice ceased. Shubha looked up at her mother-in-law. A deep frown knitting her brow, Ba stared steadily into the corner opposite. She got up and walked over, and picked up something from the floor.

'Shubha, what is this?' Ba's voice cracked. Like hard dry earth. The barren sunbaked earth cracks, willy-nilly, along deep jagged fissures. With thin trembling fingers Ba held up the burnt-out stub of a cigarette.

2 In groups of three or four, discuss why you think the discovery of Shubha's cigarette stub would have such an affect on Ba.

3 What other kinds of behaviour do you think Ba might disapprove of?

4 In your group, choose one of these ideas and represent it in the form of a still image, with one of you as Ba showing her disapproval, e.g. Ba walks into the house as Shubha is having a get together with friends and drinking alcohol.

5 Add thought tracking for each character and give your work a caption.

6 Share these with the rest of the class.

ACTIVITY B

1 Working in pairs, choose between you the most interesting idea from the starter activity. Improvise a scene in which the young person has to explain their actions to the older person, who in turn explains the reason for their disapproval.

2 Join another pair and present your scenes. Evaluate for each other how effective the characters were in expressing their differing ideas, yet maintaining a respectful approach within their characterisations.

3 In your group of four, now discuss how an adult might behave in a way that disappoints you and challenges your respect for them.

4 Choose the most interesting idea and, in pairs, improvise a scene in which you tactfully discuss their disappointing behaviour with them.

5 Present your work to the same pair you were working with in Activity B2.

Evaluate each others' work. How effective was the tactful language in maintaining the mutual respect of the relationship?

Review

- As a class discuss: How difficult is it to sustain a relationship of mutual respect between two people from different generations?
- Reflect on your own ability to use the drama techniques of still image, thought tracking, caption writing and improvisation.

Homework

- Focus on one of the improvisation ideas you have worked on in this unit and write a short playscript for two characters.

You Made Me

Aims

- To develop different interpretations of a scene.
- To analyse the language, form and dramatic impact of a scene.

Starter session

Think about what 'family' means to you. List five words you positively associate with family and five words you negatively associate with family.

Introduction

You Made Me, by Kelvin Reynolds and Adrian Lockwood, is a play about children coping with family break up in different ways. Wayne's dad now lives in a different town with his new wife and children.

Development

1 In pairs, read aloud the following extract from *You Made Me*.

MRS GOLDING	Violence is not the answer, Wayne. You should know that by now. Have you got anything to say? (**Wayne** *is silent and stares at the floor*) The boy was only in Year 8, Wayne. Do you know how much bigger you are than he is?
WAYNE	He was bugging me.
MRS GOLDING	I'm sure that he was, but there are other ways of dealing with that kind of situation.

> WAYNE   I can't do anything right, can I?
> MRS GOLDING   Well, that's really up to you, Wayne.
> WAYNE   Well, are you going to expel me or not?
> MRS GOLDING   No, Wayne. You've got one more chance.

2 Look closely at the language in the scene and think of a word that describes the atmosphere. Which uses of language create this atmosphere? Feed back your findings to the group.

3 In your pairs, create a sequence of three still images to show what happened between Wayne and the Year 8 boy. For each still image construct two lines of dialogue.

4 Now present your sequences with the dialogue.

5 Read the next part of the extract:

> WAYNE   (*Sarcastically*) Can I go now, please?
> MRS GOLDING   I think you had better. Your father is waiting outside. Please send him in, I will need to talk to him before you both leave. (*Wayne exits*)

6 Find a new partner and improvise the scene between Mrs Golding and Mr Northrop (Wayne's Dad). What atmosphere do you want to create in the scene? Make it different from the atmosphere in the scene with Wayne.

7 Now read the next extract, which is later in the car as Mr Northrop drives Wayne home.

> MR NORTHROP I can't understand why you keep doing this.
> WAYNE You don't understand anything.
> MR NORTHROP Now come on Wayne, that's not fair.
> WAYNE Oh, it isn't fair, is it? What about you letting me down all the time? How fair is that?

8 Finish the scene by writing or devising ten more lines, which create the impression that it is all Mr Northrop's fault.

9 Now develop an alternative ending to the scene that puts the blame on Wayne.

Review

- Individually, thinking back to the starter activity, list five words you think Wayne would associate with 'family'.
- As a whole class, conduct an in-role meeting. You are all experts in child behaviour and your function is to produce some guidelines for the Northrop family, which will help Wayne to deal with the break up of his family.

Homework

- Write out the main findings of the meeting and the advice given to the Northrop family.

Spitting words

Aims

- To analyse the language, form and dramatic impact of a scene from Anton Chekhov's comedy *The Proposal*.
- To recognise, evaluate and extend the skills and techniques you have developed through drama.

Starter session

- As a class, discuss the television or film characters that make you laugh.
- Try to pinpoint exactly what it is about them that is so amusing. Is it the way they speak? Is it what they say, or the way they move? Are the situations in which they find themselves absurd, or is it a combination of these factors?
- Record your group findings on a huge spider diagram around the word 'comedy'.

Introduction

Russian-born Anton Chekhov is considered to be one of the most important dramatists of all time. *The Proposal* is a short one act comedy written in the 1880s.

The play is about a landowner, Lomov, a 35-year-old hypochondriac who comes to propose marriage to a neighbouring landowner's daughter, Natalyia. However, because Lomov is so nervous he becomes sidetracked into arguing with Natalyia over a small meadow which separates their two properties.

The following extract shows the heated exchange between Lomov, Natalyia and her father, Stepan Stepanovich Choobukov.

Development

1 In groups of three, read the following extract, each taking the role of one
of the three characters:

LOMOV	No, you're simply taking me for a fool and laughing at me! You call my land yours, and then you expect me to stay cool and talk to you in the ordinary way. Good neighbours don't behave in this way, Stepan Stepanych! You're not a neighbour, you're a usurper!
CHOOBUKOV	What's that? What did you say?
NATALYIA	Papa, send the men to mow the meadows at once!
CHOOBUKOV	[to LOMOV] What was it you said, sir?
NATALYIA	The Volovyi meadows are ours, and I won't give them up. I won't, I won't!
LOMOV	We shall see about that. I'll prove to you in court that they're mine.
CHOOBUKOV	In court? You take it to court, sir, and all the rest of it! You do it! I know you – you've really just been waiting for a chance to go to law, and all that. It comes natural to you – this petty niggling. Your family always had a weakness for litigation. All of them!
LOMOV	Please don't insult my family! The Lomovs have all been honest men, and not one of them has ever been on trial for embezzling money like your uncle!
CHOOBUKOV	Every member of the Lomov family has been mad!
NATALYIA	Every one of them – every one!
CHOOBUKOV	Your grandfather was a dipsomaniac, and your youngest aunt, Nastasyia Mihailovna – yes, it's a fact – ran away with an architect, and all the rest of it. …
LOMOV	And your mother was deformed! [Clutches at his heart.] This shooting pain in my side! … The blood's gone to my head… Holy Fathers! Water!
CHOOBUKOV	Your father was a gambler and a glutton!
NATALYIA	Your aunt was a scandal-monger – and a rare one at that!
LOMOV	My left leg's paralysed… And you're an intriguer…

	Oh, my heart! ... And it's an open secret that before the elections you... There are flashes in front of my eyes... Where's my hat? ...
NATALYIA	It's mean! It's dishonest! It's perfectly vile!
CHOOBUKOV	And you're just a malicious, double-faced, mean fellow! Yes, you are!
LOMOV	Here it is, my hat...My heart...Which way do I go? Where's the door? Oh! I believe I'm dying... I've lost the use of my leg... [*Walks to the door.*]
CHOOBUKOV	[*calling after him*]. I forbid you to set foot in my house again!
NATALYIA	Take it to court! We shall see! [LOMOV *goes out staggering.*]

2 In your group, discuss which elements of the scene make it comic.

3 Look in particular at the situation, Lomov's actions and the language.

4 For each character, choose a line from the scene above that you think is the most spiteful or powerful.

5 Stand in a circle and take turns to repeat your line, making it as wounding as you can.

6 Now add an appropriate form of gesture to accompany your line, such as pointing your finger or shaking your fist, and continue repeating your line in turn around the circle.

7 Break away from your group and move around the space individually, repeating your line and gesture and adding characteristic movement.

8 Remember the following:
  – Lomov is always complaining of pain in his heart/leg
  – Natalyia is an elegant young woman
  – Choobukov is a proud older man.

9 They all have their anger in common, and it is the language they use and the absurdity of the situation that makes it comic.

10 Now watch all the Lomovs, then the Natalyias, then Choobukovs. Pinpoint those that are interesting or effective but not too overplayed.

11 Go back to your original group of three and replay the scene, remembering to include your gestures and movements and to build up the anger and tension in the scene. Think carefully about the position of your character in relation to the other characters and an audience.

Review

- Watch and evaluate each other's work. How do some groups make the comedy of the situation work?
- Consider how Natalyia might behave in the scene that follows, when she finds out that Lomov had actually come to propose marriage to her!

Don't ask me

Aims

- To explore the subject of the poem 'Don't ask me' by Jon Milos and use this as a starting point for your drama work.
- To create roles and develop techniques to help you sustain them.

Starter session

- In pairs, discuss what you care about and what you don't care about.
- Now individually select the five things you care about most and five things you care about least. Report back to your partner, who will in turn report back to the whole class.
- Report back to the class on your partner's 'cares and care nots'.

Introduction

Jon Milos is a poet from Yugoslavia. 'Don't ask me' creates a strong sense of character, which you will be building on in your drama work. As you consider the poem, remember that Yugoslavia has been broken up by numerous wars in the last decade.

Development

1 Read the poem aloud to yourself.

DON'T ASK ME

Don't ask me
Who won the first Marathon
I am not interested in sport

Don't ask me
Who dropped the first nuclear bomb
That is not my problem

Don't ask me
Who painted the Mona Lisa
I don't care for Art

Don't ask me
Who got the Nobel prize in literature this year
I am not paid for that

Don't ask me
Who wrote the ninth symphony
Music doesn't move me.

Don't ask me
Who first set foot on the moon
I couldn't care less.

Don't ask me
Who murdered Julius Caesar
It is no concern of mine

Don't ask me
I have no time for stupid things
I have got my job to do
And my family to care for
About anything else I don't give a damn.

by Jon Milos

2 Individually, think of a word to describe the character in this poem. Feed back your words to the class.

3 Who do you think the character is talking to? In pairs, create a short dialogue between the character and the person they are talking to. What is the status of the other character? Convey what the character cares about in your dialogue.

4 In groups of four, decide what are the character's strengths and weaknesses. Feed back your findings to the class.

5 Hot seat the character. One person is in role as the character from the poem; the rest of the class ask questions. Try and find out what has made the person think as they do. Can you think of any dangers in thinking in this way? You may want to challenge them with your question. Take turns asking questions and listening to the responses.

6 In your groups, think back to the starter exercise. Using still image and narration, create a visual version of the poem in which you convey your 'cares and care nots'. Use the structure of the poem to help you structure your drama work.

Review

- Debate the following: 'People should mind their own business, look after their own and to hell with the rest of the world!'.
- Consider this **polemic** and, in your groups, develop an argument in favour of or against the statement. Take it in turns to make your arguments, listening carefully to other views.
- To finish off, take a vote when all the arguments have been made.

KEY WORDS

A **polemic** is a challenging statement made to stimulate a strong response in an argument.

A *play you've seen*

Aims

- To critically evaluate a performance of a play you have seen in school or at a theatre, identifying the contributions of the writer, director and the actors.

Starter session

- Decide on a play that you have all seen. Sit in a circle and take it in turns to retell the story or narrative of the play as a whole class. Each speaker should speak for only five to ten seconds before the next person in the circle continues. Do not worry at this stage if you do not get everything in the exact order – the aim is to remember as much as possible.
- Recollect in pairs the three most impressive moments in the play. Feed back your findings to the class.

Introduction

This unit aims to build your confidence when talking and writing about performances you have seen. It will also enhance your understanding and enjoyment of plays. Many GCSE courses will expect you to see and respond to live theatre. Thinking critically about performances will also have a positive impact on your own creative drama work.

Development

1 In pairs, recreate through improvisation, or use a script if you have one, an important moment that involves one or two characters from the play. As you do so, think about how the actors used voice, movement, and gesture.

2 Decide what mood or atmosphere was created by the actors.

3 Find another pair and perform your moment to them. They will give you feed back on how you used voice, movement and gesture. Did your intentions match their feed back? Now swap over and watch the other pair's performance.

4 What were the dramatic intentions of the play? Decide in groups of four. Limit yourself to three dramatic intentions. What did the performance intend to teach the audience? What did it intend them to feel or think? Is there a message in the play? Can you think of any other reasons for or purposes of the play?

5 Who was responsible for the dramatic intentions, the writer or director? Make a list of what you think the writer's contribution to the production was and what you think the director's contribution to the production was?

6 Look at the glossary at the back of this book and identify any words that might be helpful to you in critically evaluating the performance.

Review

- In your groups, review the activities you have done in this unit and prepare a short presentation for the class. Each person in the group should participate. Use the following structure to plan your presentation:
  a We think the dramatic intentions of the play are …
  b To convey these intentions the actors …
  c We think the writer's and director's contributions were …
  d The overall impact of the performance was …
- Now rate the effectiveness of the performance out of five, five being totally effective.
- Make your presentations to the class.

Homework
Read the following notes and critical evaluation from Disney's *The Lion King*. Model your writing on this example.

Disney's Lion King, London.

Notes

Character – Scar – manipulative/scheming – nasty – lives in cave/dark and menacing – ambitious/power hungry – evil – terrifying – outcast – contrasts with good characters – Lion with human qualities/anthropomorphism – two faced – twisted – spiky hair – giant mask above head – eyebrows 'one bends up, one down' – actors face visible – resents Simba and Mustafa – comic – controls hyenas – Key moment elephant graveyard – skeletal look of steps – 'Be prepared for a new King' Scar

Example

The actor playing Scar had to create a character who contrasted completely with Mustafa, his king and brother, and Simba his nephew. It is Scar's ambition to be king that creates the drama in the piece. The actor used a giant mask above his own head to create this Lion/man character. It is called anthropomorphism when animal characters are given human qualities and characteristics.

He had spiky hair and one eyebrow pointing up and the other down. This created the impression of a twisted, pained character. Scar is portrayed as a two-faced character, sometimes seeming friendly to Simba and sometimes threatening and terrifying. The actor creates this by sometimes giving Scar slow and slumbersome movements, and at other times he moves with lightning speed. A similar contrast is used in the way voice is used to help create the two sides of Scar. One moment he is slow and comic, and moments later his voice becomes harsh and vicious.

For me, a key moment in the performance was when Scar was with the Hyenas in the elephants' graveyard and said, 'Be Prepared for a new King'. It is at this point that he appears most dangerous. His movements start to become more like the hyenas', and set and lighting combine to create a chilling effect, showing what the world of the play would be like if Scar succeeded in becoming king. The director/designer has made a clear contribution to creating this character – the mask and costume paint a picture of Scar even before a word is spoken, confirming to the audience the nature of the character. For me, this was a totally effective performance, which conveyed the dark side of humankind.

Task
Now write a critical evaluation of the live performance you have seen. What contributions did the actors, director and writer make to the overall impact of the play and how effective was it? Base your writing on the presentation you made in class.

Extension Activity
To find out more about Disney's Lion King, use a search engine to find the Lion King website.

Glossary

The glossary explains the meanings of words used in the book and provides some specialist drama and theatre terms which will help you when talking or writing about theatre.

Word	Unit	Page	Definition
Actor			A person who creates and performs characters for an audience. Can be male or female.
Action			The movements actors use to tell the story and convey character in a scene.
Anthropomorphism			Where animal characters are given human characteristics and qualities.
Aside	9.1	73	When an actor speaks in character directly to the audience without the other characters hearing.
Audience			The people who are watching a performance.
Atmosphere	9.3	79	The general feeling created for an audience by the characters.
Backstage			All the areas in a theatre that the audience do not see.
Black out			When all the theatre lights fade down to darkness, often used to show that the play is over.
Blocking			This is the process of recording and finalising the movements actors make on stage.
Closed question	8.2	45	A question that you answer 'Yes' or 'No' to.
Collaborative	7.2	14	When you work with others to create something. It suggests you work as equal partners in the process.
Chorus			An individual or group of actors who comment on the action in the play and help guide the audience's thinking on the characters and action.
Crew			People who work on technical jobs in a production.
Cross-cutting	7.9	36	When you stop the action and move back and forward across or through scenes.
Cue			This is the trigger for action. It can be a spoken word or movement.
Cyclorama			A large screen, usually upstage, onto which light is projected.
Debate	8.10	72	A formal argument in which the participants argue a point of view which may or may not be their own.

Word	Unit	Page	Definition
Devise	7.2	14	Where you create your own play for an audience without a script as a starting point.
Designer			The person who creates and co-ordinates the visual aspects of a production.
Dialogue	7.5	24	Where two or more characters are speaking in a scene.
Dilemma	8.7	61	A problem with two possible outcomes.
Director			The person with overall creative control of a play or production.
Drama skills	8.5	57	The techniques you can develop to increase your ability to convey ideas to an audience. They include: voice, movement, gesture, facial expression, pace, spacing, levels and status.
Dramatic impact	9.2	76	The effect a piece of drama has on the audience.
Dramatic intentions	8.5	57	What you intend the audience to think, feel or consider on seeing your drama.
Dramatic sequence	9.4	82	The scenes or events that make up your devised play. It suggests that one thing follows on from another.
Entrance			The way on to stage for the actors.
Exit			The way off stage for the actors.
Gels			Coloured material placed in front of a lantern to create coloured light.
Gobo			A lighting special effect used to project shapes of light on to a stage.
Fade in/Fade out			Using lighting to gradually reveal or close a scene.
Flashbacks	9.6	27	Scenes that show something that has happened in the past.
Flat			A canvass stretched over a wooden frame on which scenery can be painted.
Flying			This is the term used for dropping scenery or backdrops onto a stage from above during a performance.
Follow spot			A spotlight that can be moved to follow the action on stage.
Freeze-frame	8.3	51	See still image.
Hot seating	8.2	45	When a character or person in role sits in the hot seat and questions are fired at them. They must respond in role. It is used for deepening the understanding of the role.

Word	Unit	Page	Definition
House lights			Lights that illuminate the audience.
Improvisation	7.6	27	When you devise and present a storyline with little preparation.
Lantern			This is the technical name for a theatre light.
Lamp			This is the technical name used for the bulb that goes in a lantern.
Make-up			Pigment applied to an actor's skin, usually face, to help create a convincing characterisation for the audience.
Mime	7.7	30	A performance that conveys character and plot using movement and gesture, without the use of words.
Minimalist			Where a director and actors produce a performance using as little in the way of props, costume and scenery as possible. This forces the actors to compensate with creative use of acting skills.
Mood			The prevailing feeling associated with a situation.
Monologue	7.4	21	Where one character speaks directly to the audience.
Montage	8.5	57	When you create a series of images or scenes that contrast, challenge and encourage an audience to take a new look at the subject.
Narrative/Narration	7.3	18	The story or plot, the main events, incidents and encounters. Where a character or chorus tells the audience directly things that they will not see on stage, often used to fill in the gaps between the action.
Open question	8.2	45	A question that you cannot answer 'Yes' or 'No' to. It forces the answerer to give a more detailed response.
(A) Play			A dramatic performance in which actors take on roles and convey a story to an audience. Usually written by a playwright.
Playwright			The writer of a play.
Polemic	9.9	101	A challenging statement made to stimulate a strong response in an argument.
Point of view			Looking at a situation or characters from the perspective of another character.
Properties or props			Any objects that actors handle or use in the performance.

Word	Unit	Page	Definition
Prepared improvisation			When you are given time for rehearsal of your scene in order to present it to an audience.
Rehearse (verb) or **Rehearsal** (noun)	7.3	18	When you practise a play in preparation for presentation.
Reportage	7.10	39	When you use journalistic conventions to interpret and convey events. For example, creating a news report or writing a front page story.
Role	7.4	21	A part or character. played by an actor.
Role-on-the-wall	8.4	53	Written details of a role on a board or paper that can then be displayed on a wall for further reference.
Role-play			When you take on the part of someone else. You aim to see situations as they would and respond as they would.
Role reversal	8.5	57	When you swap roles to see the situation from another point of view.
Round	9.2	76	When you say or sing lines repeatedly.
Sound effects			Any sound created to support a performance. Can be produced live on stage or played back using electronic devices such as a mini disc.
Still image	7.1	11	When you create a frozen moment in a drama. It is often used as a starting or finishing point, or to mark an important moment. The actors should remain completely still as if the action were 'paused' on a video.
Stage areas			These terms are used to describe the different areas on a stage.

Upstage Right	Upstage Center	Upstage Left
Center Stage Right	Center Stage	Center Stage Left
Downstage Right	Downstage Center	Downstage Left

Audience

Word	Unit	Page	Definition
Staging			**Proscenium arch**. This is a picture-frame opening through which the scenery and action are viewed. The audience faces in one direction. Scene changes and performers' entrances and exits are made behind the proscenium arch, out of sight of the audience. **Open stage.** This is similar to the proscenium arch stage – the audience faces in one direction towards the stage, but there is no arch. **Thrust stage**. This is the most widely used of all theatre spaces. In the basic thrust arrangement, the audience sits on three sides, or in a semicircle, enclosing a stage which projects into the centre of the audience. Entrances and exits are made from the sides and backstage. Spectators surround the action, but scene changes and other stage effects are still possible. **Theatre-in-the-round**. This has a playing space in the centre of a square or circle, with seats for spectators surrounding it. This arrangement is similar to that in sports arenas which feature boxing or basketball. The audience sits on four sides or in a circle surrounding the stage. Entrances and exits are made through the aisles or underneath the aisles. **Traverse stage**. This has the audience seated on either side, so "the action sweeps from end to end" in the course of the play. The traverse stage allows enormous versatility in describing the way the two worlds confront, overlap and obliterate each other.
Status	8.1	43	The position of power between characters.
Sustain	8.2	35	When you maintain or remain in a role.
Strike			This is when all the elements of the production are taken down or removed from the theatre following the last performance.
Tabs			A term used to describe any curtain used on stage.
Tension			When a feeling of suspense is created for an audience who are anticipating the action ahead. Can be used to help keep an audience interested in the action.
Thought tracking	7.1	11	When you speak aloud the unspoken thoughts of a character or role.
Thought tunnel	7.7	30	When a character from the drama walks slowly between two rows of students. You link your hands together in the air to create an arch. As the character passes each student they call out what they think the character is thinking.